# THE MIKE ROY COOKBOOK NO. 2

# THE
# MIKE ROY
# COOKBOOK
## NO. 2
### EVERYDAY RECIPES

THE WARD RITCHIE PRESS · PASADENA

The material in this book is reviewed and updated
at each printing.

Ninth Printing, 1974

# Dedication

If ever a man owed a debt, the obligation I owe my listeners and readers is one which can never be repaid. The beautiful part of it is that they never bill me, giving of themselves, their affection and knowledge. I accept this in the spirit in which it is given in all humility and thankfulness. And I would presume to dedicate this volume to all of them, in love and everlasting gratefulness.

# Contents

# The Words at the Beginning

Softly now. Let us begin softly . . . and with feeling.

Any smart woman will tell you there are three ways to a man's heart. This book will deal with the second and third ways: food and booze.

But I would not presume to deal with food and booze from the viewpoint of amusement alone. Rather, I would like to relate the substance to sustenance. I would like to examine "us" for a moment. It has become necessary for us to look at all the rest of us in order that we may understand the kind of people we have become.

Dr. Ernest Dichter and his Institute of Motivational Research has conducted numerous surveys. I assume they are scientific since his organization is paid in the millions each year for guiding the marketing research of some of our largest corporations. He says we have to learn to combine our personal attitudes toward life with material things embodying them. And he kicks us around a bit when he tells us that more swear words are probably used when a needle breaks or a car fails to start than when one's very philosophy of life is challenged or disaster strikes. We are the slave of things. Shangri-La is not a spiritual heaven as much as a physical paradise where the sun shines, eternal spring calms the nerves, and, best of all, no work or struggle with safety, security or daily livelihood is necessary.

As modern life becomes more complex, says Dr. Dichter, our struggle with the world around us becomes a more and more relentless cold war. And the army of the enemy is enormous. It ranges from a blown fuse or a run in a stocking to the dirt on the floor—from a flat tire to a lost button.

Along with this tyranny of things, has come the status symbol of food and wine. Time was when man hunted to fill the larder. But now the status of the larder tells us what we are. A Frenchman, having fallen on hard times, will sell his paintings and keep his wine cellar. And if you ask him to explain his action, he will tell you: "A man can do without art but not without culture."

We acquire appetites for foods which symbolize the picture we have of ourselves. If I have recently come into a lot of money, I may become more interested in caviar and paté de foie gras than such things as bean soup, peanut butter or codfish cakes.

The variety of things now available to all of us is almost incalculable. The modern super market is loaded with items which cut across the full spectrum of the food scene. There's something there for each of us. There are those who say that we will separate into two kinds of people. Those who will deal with the new convenience foods embodying everything from TV dinners to pot roast done with onion soup mix and those who will be true food bugs and insist on creating everything from scratch according to the rules of the true gourmet. My old friend and noted authority Jim Beard, swears by the latter and yet I know many home economists who say that it will all be on the convenience side. I think neither is wholly right. We'll do a little of both.

There will be times when we want to bring out the lace cloth and the gleaming silver and entertain as regally as we can, but not every night. There are times for the TV dinner, and there are times when old fashioned bean soup and corn bread sounds mighty good.

What I would like to see is the constant and liberal application of TLC (Tender, Loving Care) applied to everything we cook. If pork chops and bean soup are on the menu, let's do them as best we can. I recommend a short cut if it makes cooking sense and doesn't ruin the recipe.

This book carries some of the best "every day" recipes I know. I've included some from my boyhood in a North Dakota small town. My wife, Alison, has allowed me to use several of her "down east" specialties. (I'll put her baked beans against any on the face of the earth, and her ginger bread formula has been known to reduce strong men to putty). I've also included many recipes for casseroles, since so many of you have asked for them.

If this is a cookbook you will keep in the kitchen, and if it becomes shortening or gravy-stained with the passage of time, then this book will be a success. For this is planned to be an eater's book for those of you whose good life partly comes from a good table.

2

# Appetizers

# The Words about Appetizers

We've reached a desperate stage in our way of life when it comes to appetizers. See if I'm not right. The next time you're invited to someone's home for dinner you'll be greeted at the door by your host and hostess. You'll be "helloed" enthusiastically with loud laughter and there'll be a four-way exchange of cheek-kissing. Then the host will say: "I'll pour your first drink and after that you're on your own. I don't intend to spend the evening mixing drinks!" And ten-to-one he'll load that first drink which is calculated to get you started, but which really is the beginning of the end. You no sooner are seated when in comes the hostess with her appetizers. Her tray will have at least three of what we have come to call dunks: rich cheese or sour cream full of clams, nuts, anchovies and some items which are new to your taste and which you, in your most polite way, must inquire about. This sends the conversation on to the topic of food, which reminds your hostess that there is more and she'll bow out gracefully and return with a couple of chafing dishes full of meatballs, hot dogs, tacos or stuffed mushrooms. You groan to yourself because you realize that there is enough food for a dinner right here and visions of bicarb start to dance in your head.

I respectfully submit that appetizers were invented to stimulate the appetite not to satiate it. All of these items are fine if you are hosting a cocktail party and you want to impress your guests with your culinary ability. But they most certainly do not belong as a prelude to a dinner.

Going back to what usually happens at that dinner party. Having made that first drink for you the host sneaks a quickie. And he follows this procedure with the arrival of each guest. You try gamely to keep up with him and the rest of the group. You partake of too many appetizers (perhaps in all honesty to put a blotter down there in those regions which need it most) and the party dawdles its way. The hostess casts anxious glances at the clock, realizing that her dinner is cooking too long in the kitchen. An hour after the appointed hour you finally sit down to dinner and discover the salad is a bit wilted and the meat is overdone. But gallantly you wade through it along with wine and after-dinner drinks. As you say good night the first rumbles begin in the vicinity of your stomach and you wend your way home to a night of acidity and floor-pacing.

So consider this a plea for judicial use of appetizers. If you are planning a standard company-type dinner, keep the appetizers to a minimum. I would suggest a bowl of cold shellfish—shrimp, lobster or crab with a simple tomato or mustard-mayonnaise sauce; with perhaps a cold platter of crunchy fresh vegetables—cauliflower, celery, etc.; and marinated small pieces of fish or cooked vegetables or I like marinated artichoke hearts or mushrooms.

Now then, since the cocktail party has become a part of the American way of life, here, for your use, are some appetizers which really are cocktail party food.

(For my North Dakota taste I like caviar with grated onion and chopped hardcooked egg and I like to drink Scotch or beer with it. What's that old saw about taking the boy out of the country but you can't take the country out of the boy?)

## COCKTAIL BALLS

It seems that man has been eating his food on a stick since time began. The custom now carried over to the cocktail hour. And here are some cocktail balls you serve on a stick (toothpick).

### HORS d'OEUVRE SAUERKRAUT BALLS

¼ pound bulk pork sausage
¼ pound cooked ground ham
¼ pound cooked corned beef, ground
¼ cup finely chopped onion
½ teaspoon finely chopped parsley

½ cup all-purpose flour
½ teaspoon salt
½ teaspoon dry mustard
1 cup milk
1 pound sauerkraut, drained and chopped fine

Combine all the ingredients and roll into small balls, a little smaller than a walnut. Dip in additional flour, then beaten egg, then in soft bread crumbs. Deep fat fry in cooking oil at 375° until golden—about six minutes. Makes about 48.

### SALMON BALLS

1 pound smoked salmon
½ pound cream cheese
1 teaspoon lemon juice
1 tablespoon light cream

Salt, pepper to taste
1 teaspoon dill weed or finely chopped fresh dill
1 teaspoon chopped chives

Grind the salmon, using the fine blade of the food chopper. Combine with the cream cheese, lemon juice, cream, chives, salt and pepper. Roll into marble-sized balls. Roll in dill weed or fresh dill. Chill and serve on picks. Makes 40-50 balls.

### CEVICHE

As modern transportation makes the world a smaller place, we're starting to broaden the base of our culinary knowhow. This Mexican appe-

---

*Boiled eggs should never be boiled, just simmered. There's no such thing as hard boiled eggs—they're hard cooked eggs.*

tizer is fast becoming a favorite. I suspect the Polynesians supplied the original in their recipe called loma loma.

1 pound boneless, skinless fish filets
1 cup lime juice (can use lemon)
2 tomatoes, peeled, seeded and chopped

1 onion finely minced
¼ cup green chiles, seeded, deveined and chopped
4 tablespoons oil
½ teaspoon each salt, pepper and oregano

Cut the fish in one-inch cubes and place in a glass or stainless steel bowl. Add the lime juice and toss well, being sure that each piece of fish is well coated with the juice. Add the other ingredients and mix well. Cover and place in refrigerator to chill at least eight hours. This will keep easily four days. Serves 8 as appetizer.

## MARINATED EGGPLANT

This has to be one of the oldest recipes from the old world. You'll probably find it claimed by the Greeks, the Armenians and the Bulgarians, not to mention a hundred nomad tribes. It was good then and it's good now. The Italians use it too. They call it Muhljohn.

1 unpeeled eggplant cut in one-inch cubes
½ cup white wine vinegar
1 teaspoon salt
½ teaspoon pepper
1 clove mashed garlic

1 teaspoon oregano
½ teaspoon sweet basil
¾ cup olive oil
(a teaspoon of dill weed gives the dish a Scandinavian flavor)

Boil eggplant in salted water to cover about ten minutes. The cubes should be soft but retain their shape. Drain. Combine other ingredients except oil. Place eggplant in a glass or stainless steel bowl and toss well with marinade and let stand overnight (at least 8 hours) in the refrigerator. Toss with oil and serve. Makes 6 to 8 servings. This will keep chilled for a week.

---

*To remove film of grease from plastic bags use powdered water conditioner only. Avoid suds which leave scum on plastic.*

8

## RED-DEVIL BALLS

1 8-ounce package cream
cheese
1 4½-ounce can deviled ham
¼ teaspoon Tabasco sauce
1½ teaspoons Worcestershire
sauce

2 tablespoons brandy
1 tablespoon grated onion
1 tablespoon chopped parsley
1 cup chopped walnuts

Combine all the ingredients except the walnuts. Refrigerate until easy to handle. Shape into small balls, roll in chopped walnuts and refrigerate just long enough to firm up again. Serve on toothpicks or with crackers. Makes about 3 dozen.

## DANISH MEAT BALLS

1 cup bread crumbs
⅓ cup milk
1 pound ground beef
¼ cup minced onion
1 egg
½ teaspoon salt
⅛ teaspoon pepper
¾ teaspoon nutmeg
(freshly grated)

¼ teaspoon allspice
2 tablespoons butter
2 tablespoons flour
½ cup beef bouillon (2 cubes)
¾ cup half-and-half
½ lemon, sliced
¼ cup sherry

Soak bread crumbs in milk. Add meat, onion, egg, salt, pepper, nutmeg and allspice and mix thoroughly and shape into balls. Place butter in pan, add meat balls and brown on all sides. Take out meat balls, add flour to pan and blend. Then add bouillon and half-and-half. Cover and simmer gravy mixture for 10 minutes. Remove cover. Add lemon slices, sherry and meat balls and simmer for 5 more minutes. Makes about 3 dozen.

## DIPS

I guess the reason for this popularity has to be the simplicity. But we've suddenly gone dip and dunk crazy. The cracker and potato chip

*Freeze chicken livers separately in meal size portions when you dress fryer. Be sure to use within three months.*

people have aided and abetted the whole thing. I rather like them and here are some that should bring you a new taste.

### PICKLE-SHRIMP DIP

½ cup chili sauce
3 tablespoons tomato paste
2 tablespoons dill-pickle liquid
1 tablespoon lemon juice
1 tablespoon prepared
  horseradish

½ cup chopped dill pickles
¾ cup chopped cooked shrimp
1 8-ounce package cream
  cheese, softened

Combine chili sauce, tomato paste, pickle liquid, lemon juice, horse-radish, pickles and shrimp; mix well. Break cream cheese into small pieces with fork. Pour pickle sauce over cheese. Serve as a dip or spread. Yield: about 2 cups dip.

### NUT DIP

1 cup peanut butter
1 pint sour cream
1 cup apple with red peel,
  grated and drained
1 tablespoon fresh horseradish

1 teaspoon hot prepared
  mustard
Parsley
Apple slices

Let peanut butter soften at room temperature. Blend all ingredients except parsley and apple slices. Chill several hours. Serve with parsley topping and apple wedges for dipping. Makes about 3 cups.

### CHEESE SPREAD

1 pound cream cheese,
  softened
½ pound Roquefort cheese, at
  room temperature
¼ pound butter or margarine,
  melted

1 medium green pepper,
  seeded and finely minced
¼ cup minced green olives
3 tablespoons minced ripe
  olives
2 tablespoons minced parsley

*Make grated chocolate for garnish by dropping chocolate bits into your nutmeat grinder—a few turns of the handle and the garnish is ready.*

| 1 teaspoon paprika | 1 teaspoon onion juice |
| 1 teaspoon Worcestershire sauce | Few drops hot pepper sauce |

Combine cream cheese and Roquefort cheese; mix well. Blend in butter. Add remaining ingredients, mixing thoroughly. Spoon into 1½-quart mold or loaf pan. Refrigerate several hours or overnight to blend flavors. Yield: about 4 cups.

### SOUR CREAM DIP

| 1 pint sour cream | ¼ pound Braunschweiger or |
| 1 package dehydrated onion soup mix | liver pate |
| | 2 teaspoons curry powder |

Mix well and refrigerate for several hours or overnight before using. Makes about 2½ cups.

### CHEESE DIPPED HOT DOGS

| ½ pound processed sharp American cheese | ½ teaspoon Worcestershire sauce |
| ¼ cup dry vermouth | 2 dozen hot dogs |
| 1 teaspoon prepared mustard | |

Melt cheese in top of double boiler and blend in wine, mustard and Worcestershire. Simmer hot dogs in boiling water for 5 minutes. Cut hot dogs in 1-inch long pieces. Spear each with a toothpick. Serve sauce in a chafing dish with water jacket. Dip the hot dogs in the sauce. Makes about 80.

### PASTRY APPETIZERS

It was the French who got it started. And now that I think about it, they had a good idea. I like those little puffs filled with all those goodies. And the nice thing about them is you can make them ahead and just heat them up.

_To keep egg yolks fresh for several days cover with cold water or salad oil and store in the refrigerator._

## PÂTÉ À CHOUX

This is a double duty recipe. It makes wonderful hors d'oeuvres and when filled with whipped cream or a sweet filling, it makes a lovely dessert.

| | |
|---|---|
| ½ cup butter | 1 cup all-purpose flour |
| ¼ teaspoon salt | 5 whole eggs |
| 1 cup boiling water | |

Add butter and salt to boiling water in the top of a double boiler. When the butter melts, add the flour all at once and stir briskly until the paste leaves the sides of the pan and forms a ball. Remove from the heat, cool slightly, and beat in the eggs, one at a time beating briskly after each addition. Force the dough through a pastry bag to form eclairs, cream puffs, or any desired shapes. To make small cocktail size puffs, drop from a teaspoon as you would cookies. Bake on a buttered baking sheet in a moderate oven (375°) for 45 minutes, or until the paste is well puffed and the cakes are dry and browned.

### FILLINGS FOR PUFFS
### (Appetizers)

| | |
|---|---|
| Avocado paste: | ¼ cup Roquefort, 1 cup avocado mashed, 1 tablespoon lemon juice. |
| Bacon & Pickle: | Combine ¼ cup cream cheese, ¼ cup mayonnaise, 3 dill pickles chopped and 6 slices crumbled crisp bacon. |
| Olive-chicken: | Combine 2 cups ground cooked chicken, ½ cup chopped ripe or stuffed olives, mayonnaise to bind, salt and pepper. |
| Crab or Lobster: | Flake 2 cups crab meat and blend it with ½ cup finely chopped celery, 1 hard-cooked egg grated, 3 tablespoons mayonnaise, ½ teaspoon Worcestershire, 2 tablespoons catsup, 1 tablespoon lemon juice, salt, pepper and a few grains of cayenne. |

*Don't throw out left over coffee. Freeze it into coffee ice cubes for use in iced coffee, same goes for iced tea.*

| | |
|---|---|
| Shrimp & Cucumber: | 2 cups minced cooked shrimp blended with 1 cup chopped cucumber, 1 tablespoon chopped chives, 2 tablespoons French dressing. Moisten with mayonnaise, salt and pepper. |
| Cheese & Anchovy: | 4 tablespoons butter blended with ½ cup grated mild cheese, 1 grated hard-cooked egg, 2 teaspoons vinegar, 1 teaspoon prepared mustard and 1 teaspoon mashed anchovy or anchovy paste. |
| Ham & Pâté: | ½ cup cooked ground ham blended with ½ cup liver pâté. |

### CHEDDAR CHEESE COOKIES

2 cups grated sharp Cheddar cheese
½ cup butter

1 cup flour
1 teaspoon salt
¾ cup finely chopped nuts

Cream the cheese and butter together. Add flour, nuts and salt. Form long rolls (about size of silver dollar). Wrap in wax paper, chill in refrigerator until ready to use. Slice thin, bake at 375° for 10 minutes on greased cookie sheet. Makes 6 dozen.

### CHEESE OLIVE SANDWICHES

1 package prepared pie pastry dough
⅔ cup grated sharp Cheddar cheese

⅔ cup chopped ripe olives
¾ teaspoon chili powder
¼ teaspoon crumbled oregano

Mix cheese and olives with chili powder and oregano. Prepare dough according to directions and roll thin. Cut with 2½-inch biscuit cutter. Put a dab of filling on half of each round, fold over in half-moon shapes. Moisten edges and pinch together to seal. Place on cookie sheets. Bake in very hot oven (475°) for 10 to 12 minutes. Serve hot. Makes about 3 dozen. Make and fill these miniature pastries ahead of time and keep in

*Dishes in which eggs have been served wash easier with small amount of salt put in them as they soak.*

the refrigerator on cookie sheets. Bake as the party progresses so you can serve them hot.

### RUMAKI

This Polynesian appetizer has become so popular that I feel it must be included. This is my personal recipe.

Chicken livers
Water chestnuts
Bacon strips
Toothpicks
¼ cup chopped green onions
½ teaspoon salt
1 cup beef consomme (canned) undiluted

½ cup red dry wine (can use sherry)
⅓ cup soy sauce
1 clove garlic, mashed
3 tablespoons lime or lemon juice
2 tablespoons brown sugar or honey

Slice chicken livers and water chestnuts in half. Sandwich a half water chestnut between two slices of chicken liver. Wrap with a half a strip of bacon and secure with a toothpick. Combine the rest of the ingredients and let the rumaki marinate overnight in the refrigerator. Broil under high heat or over charcoal until bacon is crisp.

*Slices of lemon cut through the rind and eaten with salt will kill the odor of onions on the breath.*

# Soup

# The Words about Soup

I keep thinking about words. The dictionary is full of them. It's just a matter of how they go together. Take a word like soup. There was someone way back before history who added water to meat along with some vegetables and said: "Ahah, this is soup!" And just think what we have done with the word. We speak of fog as being pea soup. If we get in trouble we are referred to as being "in the soup." When the old-fashioned bank robbers blew up the vault the nitro-explosive they used was called soup. And then there's that pie-throwing comic who calls himself "Soupy."

Personally, I think soup was created for man to invent a word such as "slurp." What else can you do with soup except slurp it? Oh, I know soup can be sipped and I do know some who drink it, but the true soup lover is a soup slurper. He's my kind of fellow. Or would you rather trade the whole thing for a "mess of potage?"

Actually, the word *soupe* (French) was not originally used to describe the liquid preparation but rather the various ingredients that went into it. Nowadays the French use the word *soupe* to describe a peasant-style soup which is rather thick in vegetables and garnished with French bread. Likewise, in the old days the name *potage* was given to dishes of meat or fish boiled with vegetables.

An interesting fellow by the name of Grimod de la Reynière put soup in its proper perspective when he said: "It is to a dinner what a portico or a peristyle is to a building; that is to say, it is not only the first part of it, but it must be devised in such a manner as to set the tone of the whole

17

banquet, in the same way as the overture of an opera announces the subject of the work." That's what I call magnificent wordage on soups. So important do the French consider their *soupe* that Prosper Montagne in his huge culinary work, *Larousse Gastronomique,* devotes some twenty-five pages to *soupe.*

I've always been a soup lover. There are times when you just can't beat a steaming bowl of mellow broth along with hot French bread and sweet country butter. Kings should fare so well. And on a hot summer day a chilled bowl of spicy coolness releases the tension and soothes a fevered, smog-kissed brow.

Here are some of the best soups in my collection—both hot and cold.

## BIG MEAL SOUP

1 package (1 lb.) dried large white navy beans
6 cups boiling water
4 cups shredded cabbage (about 1 lb.)
2 cups thinly sliced carrots (about 7 medium-size)
1 large onion, chopped (1 cup)
1 cup chopped celery
1 clove garlic, minced
1 shank end fully cooked ham, about 3 lbs.
1 package (12 oz.) smoked sausage links, sliced thin
1 can (about 1 lb.) tomatoes
1 teaspoon salt
½ teaspoon pepper
6 more cups water
1 cup elbow macaroni (half 8-oz. package)

Pick over beans, rinse, and place in a large bowl. Pour the boiling water over, cover and let stand 1 hour.

Trim several small pieces of fat from ham, melt in kettle or Dutch oven. Stir in cabbage, carrots, onion, celery and garlic; sauté slowly, stirring often, 20 minutes; remove and set aside for later use.

Pour beans and liquid into kettle; add ham, sliced sausages, tomatoes, salt, pepper, and 6 cups more water. Heat to boiling, cover, simmer 1½ hours.

Remove ham from kettle, cut meat from bone, trim off fat and dice meat. Stir into soup with vegetables. Cook 30 minutes or until beans are tender; stir in macaroni. Continue cooking 15 minutes longer, or until macaroni is tender. Ladle into a tureen or soup bowls, sprinkle with chopped parsley or Parmesan cheese, if you wish. This soup tastes even better made a day ahead and reheated. Serves 8 to 10.

## BEEF AND VEGETABLE SOUP

Alison, the wife of my acquaintance, developed this great soup meal, which only goes to prove she is of some good after all.

---

*Well scoured coffee pots makes the best flavored coffee. Wash them thoroughly in hot soap suds after each use. Once every two weeks fill the pot with water, add a teaspoon of soda (cream of tartar if aluminum) and boil ten minutes. Wash with suds.*

| | |
|---|---|
| 3 tablespoons oil | 1 cup chopped celery with |
| 1 soup bone | leaves |
| 2½ lbs. chuck, cut in small bite | 1 small yellow turnip |
| sizes | 2 sliced carrots |
| 12 cups water (3 quarts) | 1 small potato |
| ¼ cup chopped celery | 2 cups shredded cabbage |
| ¼ cup shredded parsley | 3½ cups tomatoes |
| ¼ cup chopped onion | 2 tablespoons rice |
| ½ teaspoon salt | 1 teaspoon thyme |
| ¼ teaspoon paprika | 1 teaspoon sweet basil |
| 2 tablespoons butter | 3 teaspoon Mei Yen seasoning |
| ½ cup chopped onion | powder |

Melt oil in very large heavy kettle. Add soup bone and chuck and sauté until dark brown. Pour in water. Simmer these ingredients, covered, for 2 hours. Add the ¼ cup chopped celery, parsley, ¼ cup chopped onion, salt and paprika and simmer, covered, until the meat is very tender. When meat is tender, skim fat from the stock.

Melt butter in heavy skillet. Add ½ cup chopped onion, 1 cup chopped celery with leaves, turnip, carrots, potato and cabbage and sauté for 3 minutes. Then add to stock. Also add tomatoes, rice, thyme, sweet basil and Mei Yen powder. Simmer the soup, covered, for 1 hour longer. Correct seasoning and serve. Serves 8 to 10.

### POT-AU-FEU

This is one of the great soups of the world. It literally means pot on the fire, but the French have a figurative meaning of soup pot. It's a complete meal and I'd suggest you spear out the meat, sausage and chicken and carve them before bringing to the table.

| | |
|---|---|
| 1 8-inch marrow bone, cut into | 1 2-pound broiler-fryer |
| 1-inch pieces | 4 bratwurst |
| Water | 1 onion |
| 2 pounds beef flank or chuck | 2 cloves |

*Two or three marbles in the bottom of your double boiler or your tea kettle will sound the alarm if the water gets low. They'll bang away like mad but you'll save the bottom of the pot.*

| | |
|---|---|
| 2 leeks | 1 bay leaf |
| 3 carrots, cut in 1½-inch pieces | Sprig of thyme |
| 1 medium turnip, cut in quarters | 5 sprigs parsley |
| | 6 whole peppers |
| 2 stalks celery | 1 cup dry white wine |
| ½ head cabbage, cut in wedges | Salt |

Tie marrow bone pieces in cheesecloth and place in a large kettle with water to cover. Bring to a boil, reduce heat and simmer 2 hours. Strain broth, remove bones and reserve. Add 3 quarts water to strained broth in kettle, beef, chicken and sausages. Cover and simmer 40 minutes. Add onion stuck with cloves, leeks, carrots, turnip, celery, cabbage, bay leaf, thyme, parsley and whole peppers. Partially cover and simmer 1 hour, 15 minutes. Add marrow bones and wine last few minutes of cooking. Add salt to taste. To serve, remove meats to platter and carve. Spoon broth, vegetables and a piece of marrow bone into soup bowls. Add meat to soup or serve separately. Makes 10 to 12 servings.

## BEAN SOUP

| | |
|---|---|
| 2 cups dried white beans | 1 tomato, peeled and chopped |
| 6 cups water | ½ teaspoon dried thyme |
| 1 onion, chopped | 1 tablespoon wine vinegar |
| 1 clove garlic, minced | Salt and pepper |
| 2 tablespoons olive oil | |
| 1 ham bone, or ¼ lb. diced salt pork | |

Cover washed beans with water, bring to boil and boil 2 minutes. Cover and let stand 1 hour. Cook onion and garlic in oil 5 minutes. (if you use salt pork, sauté until brown along with onion and garlic). Add to beans with remaining ingredients, except vinegar, salt and pepper. Cover and cook until beans are tender. Mash beans slightly, add vinegar and season. Makes about 1½ quarts. Serves 6.

*You'll keep the inside of your metal salt shaker top from rusting if you paint it with clear nail polish. When the lacquer is dry, use a darning needle to open the holes from the inside out.*

## ALBONDIGAS

¼ pound chorizo or other garlic-flavored sausage
1 pound lamb, ground
½ pound ground beef (chuck or round)
1 or 2 cloves garlic, crushed
1 tablespoon minced parsley
1 teaspoon salt
½ cup fine bread crumbs
1 egg, well-beaten
2 tablespoons olive oil
1 onion, sliced
1 8-ounce can tomato sauce
1 cup beer
1½ cups water

Put the sausage meat through a food grinder. Combine with the lamb and beef, garlic, parsley, salt, bread crumbs and egg, kneading with fingers to blend well. Form into balls 1¼-inch in diameter. Heat oil in skillet and brown meatballs. Remove to a casserole. Add the onion to the skillet and sauté until soft. Add the tomato sauce, beer and water, simmer until reduced and thickened. Pour over the meatballs and simmer, covered, over very low heat about 20 minutes. Serves 6.

## NEW ENGLAND CLAM CHOWDER

¼ pound diced salt pork
2 medium onions, sliced
2 tablespoons flour
½ teaspoon seasoned salt
¼ teaspoon pepper
½ teaspoon monosodium glutamate
1½ teaspoons salt
¼ teaspoon dried savory
¼ teaspoon dried thyme
Reserved clam liquid
4 medium potatoes, pared and cut into ½-inch cubes
1½ cups milk
1½ cups light cream
2 7½ ounce cans minced clams, drained (reserve liquid)
1½ teaspoons salt
1 tablespoon butter or margarine
1 tablespoon snipped parsley

In large kettle, sauté salt pork in small amount of butter, until golden. Add onions and cook until tender. Stir in flour, seasoned salt, pepper, monosodium glutamate, 1½ teaspoons salt, savory, thyme, reserved clam liquid and potatoes. Bring to boil, cover, and simmer over low heat until potatoes are tender. Meanwhile, in medium saucepan, com-

---

*There's no difference between a brown or a white egg! Buy whichever is cheaper.*

22

bine and heat just till simmering, the milk and light cream. Stir into potato mixture. Add clams and 1½ teaspoons salt, butter and parsley. Heat. Makes 8 servings.

### SPLIT PEA SOUP

1 ham bone
1 pound smoked sausage
  (salami or bologna)
½ pound split yellow dried peas
¼ pound green dried peas
6 cups water
2 large onions, cut lengthwise

¼ teaspoon thyme
¼ teaspoon savory
1 cup milk or cream
  (evaporated milk may be
  used)
1 tablespoon flour
Grated cheese

Boil ham bone, sausage and peas in water until peas are soft enough to put through sieve. Fry onions until slightly burned, add to soup along with thyme and savory. Boil for half hour, add milk and thicken with flour. Serve with grated cheese.

### CREAM OF TOMATO SOUP

¼ pound salt pork, diced
1 pound can or 2 cups peeled,
  chopped tomatoes
½ cup chopped celery
2 tablespoons chopped onion
Dash basil
2 teaspoons sugar

4 tablespoons butter or
  margarine
4 tablespoons flour
4 cups scalded milk
1 teaspoon salt
⅛ teaspoon white pepper

Render salt pork and remove crisp pieces and discard. Combine tomatoes, celery, onion, basil and sugar along with pork fat in sauce pan. Blend and simmer about 15 minutes. Press mixture through sieve or puree in blender and strain to remove seeds. Melt butter in top of double boiler over direct heat. Stir in flour. Add milk and stir and cook until smooth and thickened. Remove from heat. Slowly stir in tomato mixture. Season with salt and pepper. Cook over hot water, covered, 15 minutes. Makes 6 to 8 servings. Serve immediately and top each serving with a few croutons, if wished.

*Roast meats and poultry are better done at low temperatures. This cuts down the shrinkage and makes the meat more juicy.*

## CREAM OF CUCUMBER SOUP

| | |
|---|---|
| 3 small cucumbers | 3 teaspoons salt |
| 2 cups boiling salted water | Pepper |
| 2 tablespoons butter or | Dash cayenne |
|    margarine | 2 tablespoons sherry |
| 1½ tablespoons flour | Salted whipped cream |
| 6 cups milk | Croutons |

Peel cucumbers and slice thin. Cook in boiling salted water 10 minutes or until tender. Rub through a fine sieve, moistening with the liquid. Melt butter in a saucepan, blend in flour. Stir in milk and cook and stir until thickened. Add cucumber puree, salt and cayenne. Bring to a boil. Remove from heat and stir in sherry. Serve topped with whipped cream and croutons. Makes 6 to 8 servings.

## GREEN GAZPACHO

The cold soup idea has become a favorite starter course. One of the most popular are the Spanish Gazpachos. This recipe is deliciously different.

| | |
|---|---|
| 1 or 2 cloves garlic | 1 cucumber, peeled and diced |
| 2 slices white bread, crusts | 1 tablespoon grated onion |
|    removed | ½ teaspoon salt |
| ¼ cup Spanish olive oil | 2 tablespoons vinegar |
| 6-8 medium green tomatoes | ⅛ teaspoon cumin |
| 1 green pepper, seeded and | ½-¾ cup ice water |
|    chopped | ½-¾ cup dry white wine |

Garnishes: chopped red tomato; chopped unpeeled cucumber; chopped onion; minced hard-cooked egg; croutons fried crisp in olive oil

Put garlic through garlic press, add bread and cover with olive oil. Leave several hours or overnight. Scald tomatoes with boiling water,

---

*If the soup is too salty, don't waste it; slice a raw potato or two into the liquid. Boil for a short time and the salt flavor disappears. Remove potatoes and use for other dishes.*

24

peel off skins and cut in quarters. Combine tomatoes, green pepper, cucumber and onion and puree in electric blender a little at a time, or put through a food grinder. Combine the salt, vinegar, oil-soaked bread and cumin. Add half of this mixture at a time to the puree in the blender (or put in an electric mixer) and beat until very smooth. Chill thoroughly. Just before serving, blend in ice water and white wine to desired consistency. At table, pass garnishes to sprinkle on top of the gazpacho. Serves 4-6.

### CUCUMBER SOUP A LA SCANDIA

| | |
|---|---|
| 3 medium cucumbers | 1 teaspoon salt |
| ½ cup chopped onion | 1 cup light cream |
| 2 tablespoons butter | 2 tablespoons lemon juice |
| 2 bay leaves | ¼ teaspoon dried dill weed |
| 1 tablespoon all purpose flour | Sour cream |
| 3 cups chicken broth | |

Pare cucumbers, slice 2, add chopped onion. Cook in butter with bay leaves until tender, but not brown. Blend in flour, add broth and salt. Simmer covered for 20-30 minutes. Run mixture through a sieve. Chill well. Skim off any fat. Scoop out and discard any seed of remaining cucumber. Grate and add to chilled mixture. Add cream, lemon juice and dill weed. Serve in chilled cups with a dollop of sour cream. Sprinkle dill over top for garnish. Serves 6.

*You'll save sugar when cooking rhubarb if you add a pinch of salt to the cooking water. The salt acts as an alkaline and neutralizes the acid in the rhubarb.*

# Salad

# The Words about Salad

Along with all the other gracious gifts, a benign and loving Creator, in His infinite wisdom, provided us with the wondrous greens to fill our salad bowls. I'm sure He never intended salads to be made. A salad should be like a poem—composed.

The first great chronicle of things culinary—Brillat-Savarin—didn't devote much space to vegetables, but he made an exception when he talked about salad. "A salad" he said "freshens without enfeebling and fortifies without irritating."

Even words about salad are refreshing. Leafy heads of lettuce, in a hundred varieties, bring thoughts of cool water and rippling streams. The pungency of stringent wine vinegar lends an excitement to the salad, calmed by the soft golden oil, with herbs and spices dancing merrily amidst it all.

I realize that this description is heady, but this is my favorite food. A psychologist might find a hidden meaning in my fondness of salads. A salad is as different and original as its composer. It may be pert and saucy, or soft and soothing; it may be brave and tart, or sweet and oily. A salad changes complexion as often as a modern lady changes her hair style. Above all, a salad is personal, whether it be a simple repast in an intimate setting or a grandiose design for a formal affair. Most important, it has the touch of its architect.

As I mentioned, there may be a psychological motivation in creating a salad. Returning again to Dr. Dichter and his Motivational Research Institute, I must ask if you are one of those who refuses to eat a meal

29

without salting and peppering every item that comes from the kitchen before you've tasted it? Dr. Dichter tells us there are visual aspects of food and the way they are eaten, that are very important in our culture. Our individual way of adding ingredients or arranging food represents a most important part of it. Catsup, and many forms of seasoning such as A-1 Sauce and Tabasco, gain their major appeal because it is I, the person who eats the food, deciding how much of the condiment is added and in what manner. In some analysis of advertisements it was found that showing too much catsup on the hamburger in an ad took part of the pleasure away from a potential buyer. One of the reasons why he enjoyed catsup was his own judgment of the correct amount to add to his food. Few people like coffee with cream and sugar already added. Many people insist on buttering their own toast. Youthful rebelliousness is expressed in this way, says Dr. Dichter, concluding, "It is a revolt against mother, who used to prepare food, until one day we decided we'd had it. We could take care of ourselves."

I wonder if salad making doesn't bring one's self-assertion to a pleasant climax in the revolt against mother. I even go as far as to say that salad recipes should never be printed, though I shall forego that theory in this book. Every bowl of verdant greenery should be dressed and tossed to the complete satisfaction of its maker on an ad lib basis and with ego-maniacal satisfaction.

If you need some salad recipes, here is the way I ease my frustrations, satisfy my ego and let mother know I can do it myself.

## SALAD DRESSINGS

The secret of any salad is the dressing. I'm always reminded of the little old salad-maker, "Him," and what he told me: "Be a miser with the vinegar, and be a spendthrift with the oil." Here are some dressings and salads which I think you'll find quite different and very refreshing.

### FRENCH DRESSING

1 teaspoon salt
½ teaspoon cracked pepper
¼ teaspoon dry mustard
1 teaspoon Worcestershire sauce

¼ cup wine vinegar
1 tablespoon water
⅔ cup olive oil

Combine and shake well.

### SOUR CREAM DILL DRESSING

½ cup mayonnaise
½ cup sour cream
2 teaspoons chopped chives or green onion tops

1½ teaspoons dill weed
1½ teaspoons chopped parsley

Combine ingredients and chill.

### CUCUMBER DRESSING

1 medium size cucumber
½ cup mayonnaise
½ cup sour cream

½ teaspoon salt
Pepper to taste

Pare cucumber, remove seeds and grate on fine grater. Drain pulp. Mix grated cucumber pulp with mayonnaise, sour cream, salt and pepper; blend well. Chill until ready to use. Makes about 1½ cups dressing.

### PACIFIC SEA DRESSING (for shellfish salad)

1 pint sour cream
½ cup catsup

2 tablespoons Worcestershire sauce

*To prevent fish from sticking to the pan when frying, sprinkle a little salt in the skillet before placing the fish in it.*

31

1½ tablespoons grated onion
½ teaspoon dry mustard
1 teaspoon paprika
2 tablespoons horseradish

1 tablespoon lemon juice
2 ounces bleu cheese
¼ cup chopped green olives

Combine all ingredients and stir until blended; chill. Serve with shell-fish salad. Makes 2½-3 cups dressing.

## REMOULADE L'INDIENNE DRESSING

2 cups mayonnaise
½ cup chili sauce
4 drops (approx) Tabasco
sauce
2 teaspoons curry powder
4 anchovie filets, mashed

1 tablespoon each, chopped
fine, capers, onion, parsley,
horseradish
1 teaspoon prepared mustard
¼ teaspoon Angostura bitters

Blend well. Let stand for at least 3 hours in refrigerator.

## SALADS

Some of the items in this section you may have heard on our KNX Radio show, or have seen on our TV appearances. Some of them are released for the first time in these pages.

## COBB SALAD

This is the private recipe of my good friend, Bob Cobb, of the Hollywood Brown Derby.

1 head romaine lettuce,
chopped fine
1 head iceburg lettuce,
chopped fine
6 strips bacon, crisp and
crumbled
¼ pound Roquefort cheese,
crumbled

3 hard cooked eggs, chopped
fine
2 tomatoes, peeled, seeded
and chopped
2 avocados, chopped
¼ pound Swiss cheese, chopped
¼ cup parsley, chopped

*For best results when boiling an egg with a cracked shell, a teaspoon of salt added to the water will keep the shell intact.*

The lettuce and romaine should be chopped fine and arranged in the bottom of a salad bowl. This is the only recipe I know which requires the greens to be chopped or cut. Normally, the greens are torn to avoid bruising. The other ingredients should be chopped or diced and arranged in rows across the top of the greens so that when the salad is brought to the table, the viewer is greeted with the vari-colored rows of bacon, tomato, etc. The parsley should be sprinkled over all. At the table a ½ cup French dressing (see page 31) should be added and the salad tossed. Serves 6.

### CAESAR SALAD

There probably are as many recipes for Caesar Salad as there are chefs and head waiters in the world. I wish to include this one here because it is the original one, as given to me by Rosa Cardini, the daughter of Caesar Cardini, who originated it. Rosa says that her father's Tijuana restaurant was crowded to the walls one Sunday afternoon and his supply of food started to run low. To meet the demands of the people, he constructed the famed Caesar Salad. Incidentally, at the 1951 Culinary Convention in Paris, it was given an award as the outstanding culinary origination to come out of the Americas in fifty years. Rosa has broken the recipe into three parts, and should you want to make the original Caesar Salad, this is the way to do it.

### CAESAR OIL

¾ cup olive oil  
¾ cup vegetable oil (corn or soy)

4 or 5 medium cloves of garlic

Clean and crush garlic cloves and place in bottom of pint jar. Fill with the oils and let it stand about 3 to 4 days; no longer as it may tend to get cloudy and bitter. Strain the mixture and store the jar in refrigerator. Makes 12 ounces.

*To dredge chicken or fish with flour, put a little flour in a paper bag, drop in a few pieces of the food, and shake together thoroughly. The coating will be even and you'll use less flour.*

## CROUTONS

2 loaves white sandwich bread
1 to 2 tablespoons granulated
  garlic
1 to 2 tablespoons granulated
  onion

1 to 2 teaspoons Accent
8 ounces Caesar Oil

Keep bread about two or three days so it is easier to cut. Cut each slice 5 by 5 (25 cubes per slice). Put bread cubes in large size roasting pan. Sprinkle granulated garlic and onion, and Accent over cubes. Sprinkle in a zig zag motion the Caesar Oil across the bread cubes. Put in 225° oven. Bake 1½ hours. Shake every 4 to 5 minutes during this time to keep cubes evenly brown and dry. If desired, Parmesan cheese may be added the last five minutes. Let cubes cool. Put in jars or baggies. Cubes may be frozen for later use.

## SALAD

2 medium-size heads romaine
  lettuce
⅓ teaspoon freshly ground
  pepper
⅓ teaspoon salt
4 tablespoons imported
  Parmesan or Romano cheese
2 coddled eggs (simmered 1
  minute)

5 to 6 drops Worcestershire
  sauce
Juice of 2 fresh lemons
Few drops wine vinegar
4 oz. Caesar Oil
Croutons
¼ teaspoon dry mustard
  (optional)

Strip off top and outer leaves of lettuce and discard. Wash remaining lettuce, let drain, then wrap it in a towel. This will make it dry and crisp. Break lettuce into 2-inch strips and put in large salad bowl. Sprinkle lettuce with pepper, salt, and mustard, if desired. Add remaining ingredients, except croutons. Toss about six or seven times. Then add croutons and toss a few more times and serve immediately.

_To reuse your frying fat over and over again, add potato slices and fry until brown. The potatoes take up extraneous flavors and odors— even fish and onion._

34

## GREEN CABBAGE WITH SOUR CREAM
## & CUCUMBER DRESSING

3 cups shredded green cabbage
1 cup thick sour cream
2 tablespoons white vinegar
1 tablespoon lemon juice
1 teaspoon salt
½ teaspoon sugar

½ teaspoon paprika
3 tablespoons minced green
   onions and tops
¼ cup minced parsley
1½ cups diced green cucumber

Crisp the shredded cabbage in ice water; drain thoroughly. Blend sour cream with vinegar, lemon juice, salt, sugar, paprika. Stir in onions, parsley and cucumber. Add to bowl of shredded cabbage; toss lightly. Serves 6.


## POTATO SALAD

6 large baking potatoes
2 tablespoons oil
2 tablespoons wine vinegar
1½ teaspoons celery salt
½ cup each diced onion and
   celery
6 hard cooked eggs (optional)
½ cup mayonnaise
½ cup sour cream

2 teaspoons prepared
   mustard
1 tablespoon catsup
1½ teaspoons Worcestershire
   sauce
1½ teaspoons paprika
Salt and pepper to taste
¼ cup chopped parsley

Boil potatoes in their skins until they pierce easily with a fork. Drain. While potatoes are still hot, and handling them with several layers of paper towels or hot pads, remove peels and quarter. Season them with the oil and vinegar and celery salt. Let them chill, tossing them several times. Dice the potatoes and add the rest of the ingredients, tossing well. (4 of the eggs can be chopped into the salad and the remaining two eggs sliced and used as garnish.) The salad can be sprinkled with paprika and chopped parsley as you wish.

---

*French bread, rolls and muffins can be restored to fresh-baked if you place them in a brown paper bag with a half teaspoon of water and heat in the oven.*

## MACARONI SALAD

Women tell me they just can't make a good macaroni salad. We're particularly fond of this recipe and I think the secret rests with the French dressing over the hot macaroni.

| | |
|---|---|
| 2 cups elbow macaroni, or shells | ¼ cup each finely chopped onion and celery |
| ½ cup French dressing | ½ cup mayonnaise |
| ¼ cup sweet pickle relish | ¼ cup chili sauce |
| 2 tablespoons chopped capers | 1½ teaspoons prepared mustard |
| ¼ cup sliced stuffed olives | |
| 2 tablespoons chopped dill pickles | 1½ teaspoons Worcestershire sauce |

Boil macaroni according to directions on package. Drain well and toss immediately with French dressing. Let chill three hours, tossing several times. Add remaining ingredients and chill three hours. Serves 6.

## CRAZY SALAD

This one I leave to you. I discovered this when a listener to our radio show asked for the recipe. I confessed I had never heard of it and three good homemakers submitted recipes. Mrs. Brace, Mrs. Foresee and Mrs. Benson came to the rescue. It didn't sound good to me when I heard it and it didn't taste good to me when I made it. It's just crazy enough to include, and you might like it.

| | |
|---|---|
| 1 #2 can sauerkraut | 1 cup sugar |
| 1 cup chopped celery | ½ cup vinegar |
| 1 medium onion, chopped | 1 cup salad oil |
| 1 small pimiento, chopped | Salt to taste |

Place kraut in a strainer and pour boiling water over it. Let it drain and cool. Add the rest of the ingredients. Refrigerate, covered, 24 hours; stir occasionally. This will keep indefinitely. Use as a relish for lamb or poultry. Serves 6 to 8.

---

*To clean an enameled saucepan, fill it with cold water and three tablespoons of salt and let it stand overnight. In the morning, bring the water slowly to a boil.*

## OLD FASHIONED PERFECTION SALAD

This is an old favorite from my North Dakota church social days, and an authentic recipe.

| | |
|---|---|
| 2 envelopes unflavored gelatin | 2 cups shredded cabbage |
| ½ cup sugar | 1 cup chopped celery |
| 1 teaspoon salt | ½ cup chopped green pepper |
| 1½ cups cold water | ¼ cup chopped pimiento |
| 1½ cups boiling water | 1 cup small cooked carrots |
| ½ cup lemon juice | French dressing |
| 6 stuffed olives, sliced | Ripe olives |

Blend gelatin, sugar and salt. Add ½ cup cold water and let stand until the gelatin softens. Add boiling water, stir until gelatin dissolves. Stir in remaining cold water and lemon juice; cool. Place sliced stuffed olives in design in 6-cup ring mold. Spoon part of gelatin over to cover, chill until set. Blend cabbage, celery, green pepper and pimiento into rest of gelatin, turn into mold, chill until set. Unmold, fill center with carrots marinated in french dressing, ring with ripe olives. Makes 10 servings.

## FOUR BEAN SALAD

| | |
|---|---|
| 2 cups canned kidney beans, heated | 1 large Bermuda onion |
| 2 cups whole cooked green beans | 1 cup chopped celery hearts and leaves |
| 2 cups Italian style beans | 1 cup sour cream |
| 2 cups baby lima beans | Crisp lettuce |
| 1 cup French dressing | 1 bell pepper |
| | 12 large stuffed olives |

Drain kidney beans and mix with other beans while still hot. Pour French dressing over all. Slice the onion, remove the outer rings and save for garnish. Chop the onion centers and add to beans. Allow to marinate and chill for 2 hours. Then add celery. Add sour cream and mix well. Arrange lettuce leaves in large salad bowl and add beans. Make rings of bell pepper and use for garnish along with onion rings and olives, which have been sliced cross-wise. Serves 12.

---

*Sticky dates, figs or raisins will come apart easily if you put them in the oven for a few minutes.*

## THE EXOTICS

There comes that special time and special occasion when you want to do something a bit different with a salad. Here are some of the prettiest salads I know.

### LOBSTER IN MELON SALAD

1 melon (honeydew, Casaba, or Crenshaw)
Cold cooked lobster (about 2 pounds)
½ cup mayonnaise
1 tablespoon lemon juice
½ teaspoon salt
Gin to thin

Very carefully, cut the top off the melon. You will use it later as a cover. Scoop out the seeds and with a melon ball knife, remove the melon meat. Cut the lobster in bite-size pieces and mix with melon balls. Add the lemon juice to the mayonnaise and thin the mixture to a consistency of cream, with gin. Salt. Mix dressing with lobster and melon and return to the melon shell. Cover with the lid and refrigerate 8 hours. Serve on a large round platter surrounded with cracked ice and garnish. More lobster than melon should be in the mixture. Serves 6 to 8.

### TOMATO ROSE SALAD

4 medium-sized tomatoes
1 small cucumber
½ cup chopped celery
2 hard cooked eggs, chopped
½ cup ground boiled or baked ham
2 tablespoons chopped chives or onions
½ cup mayonnaise
Dash of salt

Peel tomatoes; cut almost thru three times to form six petals. Score cucumber length-wise with tines of fork; slice. Place tomatoes in lettuce cups; insert cucumber slice between each of the petals. Combine remaining ingredients; fill tomatoes. Pass additional mayonnaise. Serves 4.

---

*When you have to cut marshmallows, use a pair of scissors dipped in hot water.*

## ANDALUSIAN RICE SALAD

| | |
|---|---|
| 1 cup French dressing | 2 drained canned pimientos, |
| 1 clove garlic | cut in strips |
| 1 medium onion, thinly sliced | 3 cups cooked rice |
| 4 large tomatoes, thickly sliced | ½ cup minced parsley |
| or quartered | |

Mash the garlic in a salad bowl and add the French dressing. Beat to blend well. Add the onion, tomatoes and pimientos. Marinate until serving time, then toss with rice and parsley. Serve on lettuce. Serves 4.

## BEAN SPROUT SALAD

| | |
|---|---|
| 1 pound bean sprouts | 3 tablespoons minced green |
| 3 tablespoons soy sauce | onion |
| 3 tablespoons sherry wine | 1 teaspoon grated fresh ginger |
| 3 tablespoons lime juice | ¼ cup slivered almonds |
| ⅔ cup salad oil | |

Make dressing of all ingredients and pour over raw bean sprouts. Mix well. Top with toasted slivered almonds. Allow to stand a few hours before serving. Serves 8.

I have always been most fortunate in having friends who know good food and who care. One such is Mrs. Lud Gluskin, whose husband's work is well known in music cricles throughout the world. When her children matured and she and Lud decided to move to an apartment, I fell heir to her recipes. Here are two of her excellent salads.

## ORANGES AND CUCUMBERS IN SOUR CREAM

| | |
|---|---|
| 1 cup sour cream | Small clove of garlic, crushed |
| 1 tablespoon finely chopped | 3 oranges, peeled, seeded, and |
| fresh mint | cut into chunks |
| ½ teaspoon salt | 1 cucumber, pared and thinly |
| ½ teaspoon sugar | sliced |

*To skin tomatoes easily, immerse in hot boiling water for a couple of minutes, or place them on a two-tined fork and hold over an open flame until the skin breaks.*

Combine all ingredients and chill thoroughly. Serve on salad greens, garnished with mint sprigs. Serves 4.

### ORANGE AND SPINACH SALAD

5 slices bacon, crisp and well
  drained
2 tablespoons bacon fat
3 tablespoons lemon juice
2 tablespoons salad oil
1 tablespoon sugar
½ teaspoon each fresh tarragon
  and salt

1 pound spinach
1 cup sliced green onions
1½ cups thinly sliced celery
3 oranges, peeled, seeded and
  cut into small pieces
Pepper

To the 2 tablespoons of bacon fat in a skillet add the lemon juice, salad oil, sugar, tarragon and salt and bring to a boil. Wash, dry and tear the spinach and combine in a salad bowl with the green onions and the celery. Pour the hot sauce over the vegetables and toss well. Add the oranges and the bacon, crumbled, and toss lightly. Sprinkle with freshly ground black pepper. Serve immediately. Serves 4 to 6.

For those of you who want an especially nice chicken salad, and those of you who like nice cold pieces for your Thanksgiving table, the following three recipes should fill the bill.

### CHICKEN HAWAIIAN SALAD

2 cups cooked chicken, diced
½ cup finely diced celery
3 hard cooked eggs, diced
½ cup sliced almonds
½ cup Thompson seedless
  grapes

½ cup sliced ripe olives
¼ cup chopped green onion,
  including stems

Toss all ingredients well. Serve with Remoulade L'Indienne Dressing (See page 32) and garnish. Serves 4.

*To measure shortening use a cup that will hold twice as much as you need; fill the cup half full of water, add shortening till water reaches the top.*

40

## CRANBERRY FRUIT MOLD

2 packages strawberry gelatin
2 cups hot water
1 can cranberry jellied sauce
2 medium oranges, ground in
meat grinder, pulp and juice
(very fine grater)

1 medium apple, ground (pare
skin and core first)
1 small can pineapple, crushed
(juice too, if desired)

Dissolve gelatin in hot water and set to partially chill in refrigerator. Melt cranberry sauce and add to gelatin. Gelatin should chill to consistency of egg white. Grind oranges and apple and add to gelatin. Add pineapple. (Juice of canned pineapple may be used in place of one cup of the hot water, in which case dissolve gelatin in one cup of hot water and add the juice.) Place in mold and chill. Serves 8 to 10.

## CRANBERRY-ORANGE-NUT RELISH

2 cups fresh cranberries
1 orange, quartered
½ cup seedless raisins

¾ cup sugar
1 cup chopped walnuts
3 teaspoons Curaçao

Put cranberries, orange and raisins through food chopper. Add rest of ingredients. Mix thoroughly. Chill before serving. Serves 8 to 10.

41

# Meat

# The Words about Meat

"If you like rare steak, the reason could very well be that it is the strength of the bull that you are trying to incorporate." That's a direct quote from Dr. Dichter who hastens to accent his point by saying that many Americans do not like to eat lamb. One of his studies showed that a lamb is a loveable animal, but also meek. If we eat it, some of its cowardliness and "sheeplike" qualities might become ours. In Australia, however, sheep are considered manly and virile because they represent the backbone of the country's economy. Therefore, the Australians are not negatively disposed toward mutton. The cooking world is full of old wives' tales and superstitions—many of them handed down from generation to generation. I've been fascinated by a study done at New Mexico State Teacher's College which showed that 59% of all the people there, and 32% of the teachers, believed that eating fish improved the mind. Old Indian lore tells us that rabbit meat makes us timid. Some peoples believe that the occasional eating of bitter herbs will placate the gods and diminish the bitterness of life. Apropos of this, Dr. Dichter tells us that the eating of distasteful foods takes on the significance of a sacrifice. While his conclusions explain some food fanaticism as well as phobias we hope they don't apply to us personally! One thing fairly evident is that beef is man's meat. I once knew a man who didn't like steak. Nothing ever happened to him.

> Some hae meat and canna eat,
> And some wad eat that want it;
> But we hae meat, and we can eat,
> And sae the Lord be thankit.
>                     (Old Scotch-English verse)

45

Glory be, we have meat, all kinds of meat. There is veal, and pork and lamb and beef—the finest produced on the face of the earth. If America is a melting pot, we have the material to put in it. We have pots, we have broilers and barbecues and roasters and fryers. We have gas and electricity and oil and coal. God grant us the common sense to cook right.

And Sae the Lord be Thankit.

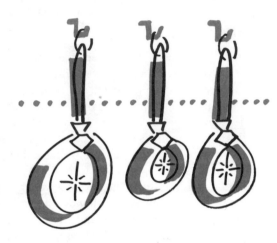

## BRACIOLE

1 large round steak about
  ½-inch thick
½ pound ground lean beef
4 slices bread
2 eggs
2 tablespoons grated Romano
  cheese (or Parmesan)
Salt and pepper to taste
¼ teaspoon nutmeg
2 tablespoons chopped parsley

2 slices lean bacon
4 hard cooked eggs
3 slices salami
3 slices Provolone cheese
2 tablespoons olive oil
1 onion (chopped)
½ cup dry, red wine
2 8-ounce cans tomato sauce
1 package frozen peas

Soak bread in water and squeeze dry; add to chopped meat. Add eggs, grated cheese, salt, pepper, nutmeg and parsley. Mix thoroughly until well blended. Cut bacon into pieces about 1-inch wide. Slice hard cooked eggs, salami and Provolone into julienne strips or slivers. Pound the round steak well. Spread it with the ground meat mixture leaving about a ½-inch rim. Place the julienne on top of the ground mixture. Roll the whole thing as you would a jelly roll and tie it well with a string. Heat the oil in a Dutch oven. Add the onions and the steak and brown the meat well. Add the wine and let it reduce by about half. Add salt and pepper and the tomato sauce. Add enough water to cover the meat. Cover the kettle and let it simmer for an hour. Add the peas and cook fifteen minutes more. When meat is done and peas are tender, remove the meat to a hot serving platter. Cut the strings and remove. Cut serving slices sidewise and dress with tomato sauce with peas. Serves 6 to 8.

## BEEF STROGANOFF

2 pounds beef filet
¼ cup flour
1 teaspoon salt
½ teaspoon pepper
1 tablespoon olive oil
1 tablespoon butter
1 tablespoon chopped shallot
  (or 1 tablespoon onion and
  ½ clove garlic, chopped)

4 ounces sliced mushrooms
1 tablespoon paprika
¼ cup brandy
½ cup beef stock (canned or
  cube dissolved in hot water)
1 teaspoon lemon juice
1 cup sour cream

*Pour salt in the oven under baking tins to prevent scorching.*

Add salt and pepper to flour. Cut beef in strips ¼ x ½ x 1½-inches and dust with the seasoned flour. Heat oil and butter in sauté pan and add floured beef along with shallot and mushrooms. Let brown and sprinkle with paprika. Add the brandy, let heat and set aflame. When flame dies, add the stock and bring to a boil. Add the lemon juice. Remove pan from heat and let cool about a half-minute. Blend in sour cream. Serve over noodles. Serves 4.

You may use round steak or stewing meat. If you do, follow the above procedure to the point where you add the stock and lemon juice. Then let it simmer for 45 minutes before proceeding as above.

### SHORT RIBS

2 pounds lean short ribs  
¼ cup flour  
1 teaspoon salt  
½ teaspoon pepper  
2 teaspoons paprika  
2 tablespoons olive oil  
2 tablespoons butter  
1 cup each, finely chopped onion, carrot and celery  
1 tomato, peeled and cut in eights  

1 clove garlic, mashed  
1 bay leaf  
¼ teaspoon each thyme and oregano  
1½ cups beef or bouillon stock  
½ cup dry red wine  
2 tablespoons cornstarch  
½ cup water  

Combine the flour, salt, pepper and paprika and dust the short ribs lightly with the mixture. Butter a Dutch oven and add all the vegetables and spices. Place the ribs on top of the vegetables. Place the kettle, uncovered, in a 450° oven and allow the vegetables and meat to brown, shaking the kettle occasionally (takes about 45 minutes to brown). Add the stock and wine. Cover the kettle tightly. Reduce the temperature to 350° and cook until the ribs are tender—about 2 hours. When ribs are done, remove them to a hot platter. Take the bay leaf out of the juice and make a puree of the vegetables in a blender, or by forcing through a sieve. Add the puree to the stock. Combine the cornstarch and water and shake well. Bring the puree-stock mixture to a boil and thicken to desired consistency with the cornstarch. Serve the gravy with the ribs. Serves 6.

---

*To clean a greasy iron pan, put salt in the pan and wipe with paper.*

## FLANK STEAK

1 cup fine dry bread crumbs
⅓ to ½ cup grated Romano
    or Parmesan cheese
2 tablespoons finely chopped
    parsley
¾ teaspoon salt
⅛ teaspoon pepper
2 eggs, beaten

2 tablespoons milk
1 (1½ pound) flank steak,
    tenderized and cut in 4 pieces
1 clove garlic, finely chopped
    or ¼ teaspoon garlic salt
¼ cup olive oil
½ cup California sherry or
    Marsala

Combine bread crumbs, cheese, parsley, salt and pepper; mix well. Combine beaten eggs with milk. Dip meat in egg mixture, then in bread mixture; repeat until all eggs and crumbs are used. Cook garlic in oil. Brown meat slowly in seasoned oil. When well browned, lower heat and add wine. Cover and simmer 30 minutes, or until tender. Serves 4.

## CHICKEN FRIED STEAK

Allow ¼ pound round steak per serving. Make a seasoned dredge of:

1 cup flour
1 teaspoon salt

½ teaspoon pepper
1 teaspoon paprika

Dredge meat pieces and pound them flat.

1 tablespoon butter
2 tablespoons oil
½ cup chopped onion
Clove of garlic, minced
1 cup beer
1 cup consomme or a beef
    bouillon cube dissolved
    in 1 cup warm water

1½ teaspoons Worcestershire
¼ cup tomato juice, or
    1 tablespoon tomato paste, or
    2 tablespoons catsup

Yield for 2 pounds steak.

Melt butter and add oil. Add meat pieces and brown thoroughly on both sides. Add the onions the last 3 or 4 minutes of browning so that they just cook to the golden stage. Add the other ingredients. Cover. Reduce fire to simmer and cook 1 hour or until meat is tender.

*Be sure to keep the baking powder dry, lest it lose its leavening.*

## BEEF STEW IN PUMPKIN SHELL

3 cloves garlic, quartered
3 tablespoons fat
2 large onions, chopped
2 large tomatoes, chopped
1 large green pepper, chopped
2 pounds tender beef, cut in
   1-inch cubes
1½ teaspoons salt
½ teaspoon pepper
1 teaspoon sugar
8 dried peach halves

3 medium-size white potatoes,
   pared and diced
3 small sweet potatoes,
   pared and diced
2 packages frozen whole
   kernel corn
2 cups beef broth or consomme
½ cup Madeira wine
1 medium pumpkin
1 tablespoon melted butter
½ teaspoon salt

Brown garlic in fat; remove and discard. Cook onion in remaining fat until yellow. Add tomatoes, green pepper, beef, salt, pepper and sugar. Mix thoroughly and simmer for 20 minutes, stirring occasionally. Add peaches, potatoes, corn and broth to meat mixture. Cover; simmer for 40 minutes. (Add more broth during cooking if needed.) Add wine.

Cut top from pumpkin and save. Remove seeds and membranes. Coat inside of pumpkin with butter and salt. Pour stew into pumpkin shell. Replace pumpkin top. Place filled pumpkin on shallow baking pan and bake in a 325° oven until pumpkin meat is tender. Place pumpkin on bed of green leaves for garnish. In serving scoop out a spoonful of the pumpkin along with the stew. Serves 6.


## SAUERBRATEN

1 cup red wine vinegar
½ cup cider vinegar
½ cup Burgundy
2 onions, sliced
1 carrot, sliced
1 stalk celery, chopped
Few sprigs parsley
1 bay leaf
2 whole allspice

4 whole cloves
1 tablespoon salt
1 tablespoon pepper
4 pound chuck pot roast
⅓ cup shortening or salad oil
6 tablespoons unsifted
   all-purpose flour
1 tablespoon sugar
½ cup crushed gingersnaps

*Stagger pans on the oven rack to provide best heat circulation.*

In large glass or china bowl combine vinegars, Burgundy, onion, carrot, celery, parsley, bay leaf, allspice, cloves, salt and pepper. Wipe meat with damp cloth; add meat to marinade. Refrigerate, covered, 3 days, turning several times to marinate evenly. Remove meat from marinade; wipe dry.

Heat marinade in small saucepan. Heat Dutch Oven or large, heavy skillet very slowly; add shortening, and heat. Dredge meat in 2 tablespoons flour, brown very well on all sides in hot fat. Pour in marinade; simmer meat, covered, 2½ to 3 hours, or until tender. Then strain liquid from meat, into 1-quart measure; skim fat from surface; measure 3½ cups liquid into saucepan; heat.

In small bowl, make paste of ½ cup cold water, rest of flour and sugar. Stir into liquid; bring to boiling point, stirring. Add gingersnaps. Pour over meat; simmer, covered, 20 minutes. Remove meat to heated platter; pour some of the gravy over it. Serve in thin slices with additional gravy. Serves 8-10.


### BEEF JERKY

This one fills a lot of requests.

| | |
|---|---|
| 3 pounds lean beef | ½ teaspoon pepper |
| 1 tablespoon salt | ⅓ cup Worcestershire |
| 1 teaspoon onion powder | ¼ cup soy sauce |
| 1 teaspoon garlic powder | |

Cut beef in strips ½-inch wide, ¼-inch thick and 4 to 6 inches long. Mix salt, onion and garlic powders, pepper, Worcestershire and soy sauce. Pour over meat strips. (For less highly seasoned jerky, use only salt). Marinate overnight in refrigerator, stirring once or twice gently. Drain and pat dry on paper towel. Dry in sun (or gas oven) until quite dry and brittle. Store in covered jar or sealed pastic bag.

*To dry in sun*: Place cheesecloth over oven or barbeque grids and arrange meat across grids without overlapping or place over open end of large foil-lined carton or over barbeque grill in direct sun. (Foil

*Don't wash eggs before storing—washing destroys their protective film.*

reflects heat). Cover with a fine wire screen to keep out insects. Secure screen in place with wire or cord so it does not touch meat. Cover drier, or place meat under shelter at night so meat does not absorb moisture from air.

*To dry in oven*: Temperature from pilot flame will dry jerky in about 4 days. Cover oven grids with cheesecloth and proceed as directed.

### CANNELONI

¼ pound veal, cut in ½-inch cubes
½ pound beef, cut in ½-inch cubes
¼ cup chopped onion
1 garlic clove, minced
½ teaspoon lemon peel
2 tablespoons butter or margarine
1 10-ounce package frozen

chopped spinach, cooked and drained
Dash thyme
Dash pepper
½ teaspoon salt
2 beaten eggs
16 crepes, cooked
1½ cups spaghetti sauce (See page 59)
½ cup Parmesan cheese

Cook first six ingredients together for 20 minutes. Add spinach and put mixture through the fine blade of a meat grinder. Season with thyme, pepper and salt. Add eggs; mix well. Put mixture in a pastry bag and fill each crepe and roll. Arrange side by side in a 10 x 6 x 1½-inch baking dish seam side down. Cover with spaghetti sauce. Bake in 350° oven 10 minutes. Sprinkle with cheese and brown under broiler for 2 minutes. Serves 8.

### CREPES

6 eggs
4 tablespoons twice-sifted flour

2 tablespoons (or more) cold water
¼ teaspoon salt

Place in mixing bowl and beat vigorously to consistency of heavy cream. Butter a small frying pan with a piece of butter about the size of a small

---

*To easily remove the shells from hard cooked eggs, use salt in the water and quickly rinse them in cold water.*

walnut and when butter begins to bubble, pour in enough batter (about a tablespoon) to cover bottom of pan with thin layer. Rotate the pan quickly to spread the batter as thin as possible. Brown, flip over and brown other side. Stack the crepes flat until all are baked. Makes 16. Or use prepared pancake mix, following instructions for thin pancakes.

## MEAT LOAF IN SOUR DOUGH BREAD

1 round loaf sour dough bread,
   unsliced

Cut off top and reserve. Wtih a sharp knife cut out the doughy part of the loaf, leaving about ½" thickness, including the crust, on the sides and bottom. Brush the insides of the loaf and inside of top with melted butter and place under broiler until insides are crispy and golden.

| | |
|---|---|
| 1¼ pounds ground chuck | ½ teaspoon black pepper |
| ¼ pound lean ground pork | ½ teaspoon thyme, or oregano, |
| ¼ pound ground veal |   or ground coriander |
| 2 slices white bread | 1 tablespoon ketchup |
| ¼ cup liquid (water, milk, | 1 teaspoon Worcestershire |
|   Burgundy, vermouth or | Sweet pickles |
|   sherry) | Sliced hard cooked eggs |
| 1½ teaspoons salt | Crumbled Roquefort cheese |

Soak white bread slices in liquid and squeeze dry. Add bread and rest of ingredients to meat and work well with hands.

Fill the crust ⅓ full with meat loaf mixture, then add a layer of sliced sweet pickles, sliced hard cooked eggs, and crumbled Roquefort cheese. Add remaining meat loaf mixture, secure the cover to the loaf with toothpicks and bake in 325° oven for 1½ hours. Slice sections across for serving. Serves 8.

---

*Use the liquid from canned vegetables in soups, sauces, stews, etc., and for making white sauce.*

## CROWD BURGERS

Allow one pound of ground
chuck for each 5 burgers
1 tablespoon oil
1 teaspoon salt
½ teaspoon pepper
1 tablespoon mustard
2 tablespoons catsup
2 tablespoons finely chopped
raw onion

2 tablespoons finely chopped
dill pickle
5 hamburger buns
5 pieces processed American
cheese
5 pieces aluminum foil,
10-inches square

Sauté the beef in the oil, seasoned with salt and pepper, until it is brown
and the liquid has cooked out. (If you wish you may add herbs such as
cumin, thyme or oregano.) Let mixture cool. Blend in the mustard,
catsup, pickle and onion. Spoon on bottom half of buns. Top with
cheese slice and top of bun. Wrap in foil and store in refrigerator until
ready to heat. Place in 350° oven for 25 minutes. Unwrap sandwiches
and serve.


### RED FLANNEL HASH

½ pound salt pork, finely diced
Butter
1 large onion, chopped
6 cooked finely diced potatoes
8 cooked finely diced beets

2 cups diced cooked corned
beef
Salt, pepper and nutmeg to taste
1 poached egg for each portion

Render the salt pork until soft. Add butter to pan and onions. Cook
until transparent. Add potatoes, beets and corned beef to the pan along
with the seasonings. Blend well. Pack the hash firmly with a spatula.
Cover and cook slowly until hash is brown on bottom. Fold half the
hash over the other half like an omelette and serve on a heated platter,
garnished with a poached egg for each portion. Serves 6-8.


### CHERRY LOIN ROAST

Pretty glazed roast. Serve with sweet potatoes and asparagus.

---

*Salt added to grapefruit sweetens it.*

54

4 to 5 pounds pork loin roast  ½ teaspoon ground cloves
  (loin end)  ¼ teaspoon pepper
1 teaspoon salt  ½ cup cherry preserves

Place roast fat side up on rack in shallow pan. Insert meat thermometer in center of roast not touching the bone. Roast uncovered in slow oven (325°), allowing 30 to 35 minutes per pound, or until thermometer registers 185°. Thirty minutes before roast is done, sprinkle with salt, cloves and pepper. Spread cherry preserves, about ½-inch thick, over top. Continue roasting until done. Makes 8 servings.


## OLD FASHIONED HAM LOAF

2 eggs  ½ teaspoon pepper
1 cup fluid, liquefied non-fat  1 pound ground chuck
  dry, or diluted  1 pound ground shoulder pork
  evaporated milk  ½ pound ground smoked ham
2 cups soft bread crumbs  1 #2 can tomatoes
  (fresh bread)    (2½ cups)
2 teaspoons salt

In bowl, beat eggs; stir in milk, crumbs, salt and pepper; let stand until crumbs are soft. Mix in rest of ingredients. Pack into greased 10x5x3″ loaf pan. Score top of loaf. Bake 1¼ hours at 350°; pour off liquid around loaf; bake 15 minutes longer. Let stand few minutes; loosen around edges. With 2 broad spatulas, lift meat loaf onto platter. Garnish with parsley. Cut into thick slices; then halve lengthwise. Makes 8 servings.


## CRANBERRY PORK CHOPS

Flour  ½ cup crushed pineapple
4 pork chops    (optional)
1 cup jellied cranberry sauce  ¼ cup water
1 teaspoon grated orange peel

Flour chops and brown in a little hot fat in skillet. Mix cranberry sauce, orange peel, pineapple and water and pour over chops. Cover and simmer 1 hour, or until fork-tender. Makes 4 servings.

*You can substitue flour for cornstarch; you need twice as much.*

55

## STUFFED PORK CHOPS

⅓ cup sesame seeds  
4 slices bacon  
⅓ cup chopped green pepper  
½ cup chopped celery  
2 cups toasted bread cubes  
2½ teaspoons pork seasoning  
    blend  

½ cup milk  
12 thin pork chops  
Salt and pepper  
⅓ cup water  

Toast sesame seeds in skillet over low heat, stirring frequently until golden brown. Place in large mixing bowl. Fry bacon until crisp and drain on absorbent paper. Pour off all but 1 tablespoon bacon drippings. Add green pepper and celery and sauté until tender. Add to sesame seeds, along with crumbled bacon, bread cubes, seasoning blend and milk. Mix until well moistened. Place stuffing on half the chops. Cover with remaining chops and fasten with skewers and string. Brown chops on both sides. Sprinkle with salt and pepper. Add water, cover and simmer 1 hour, 15 minutes or until tender. Makes 6 servings.

## HAM STEAK WITH CHERRIES

2 slices ham (¾ inch thick)  
3 cups Bing cherries  
½ cup water  
1 tablespoon chopped candied  
    ginger  

2 tablespoons sugar  
⅛ teaspoon salt  
1 tablespoon flour, in  
2 tablespoons water  

Trim fat from ham and score edges. Pit cherries and cook in water until juices run. Pile cherries on ham slices. To the juices, add ginger, sugar, salt and flour that has been mixed with water. Cook until thick and pour over ham. Bake 1 hour at 350°. Serves 6.

## APPLEJACK PORK SAUSAGES

Pork sausages  
Apple cider  
¼ cup applejack brandy  

Fresh apple slices (optional)  
Prunes (optional)  

*A small stiff brush is best for removing the corn silks from the ear.*

In the blazer of the chafing dish, cover pork sausages with apple cider. Light burner and bring to a boil. Let simmer until sausages are done and swell to about double in size (about 12 minutes). Pour off juice. Let sausages brown gently in their own fat just enough so that they don't shrink. Add applejack brandy to the pan and flame. When flame dies, sausages are ready to serve. Slices of fresh apple and prunes may be added when sausages begin to brown.

### ARMENIAN LAMB SHANKS

6 lamb shanks
2 tablespoons oil
½ cup each finely diced carrot, celery and onion
2 cloves garlic, mashed
2 tablespoons parsley
1 teaspoon salt
½ teaspoon black pepper

½ teaspoon dry mustard
1 teaspoon paprika
½ teaspoon thyme
2 tablespoons oil
1 cup bouillon or stock
1 8-ounce can tomato sauce
½ cup dry vermouth

Sprinkle half the oil in a roasting pan which can be covered. Place the celery, onion, carrots, garlic and parsley as a bed on the bottom of the pan. Skin the felt from the lamb shanks and sprinkle them with salt, pepper, mustard, paprika and thyme. Place in 450° oven for about 40 minutes. Shake the pan every five minutes and get the vegetables and the lamb shanks dark brown. Add the liquids. Cover and reduce the oven heat to 325°. Let braise or simmer about 3 hours, or until tender. Serve over rice with generous portions of the broth and vegetables. Serves 6.

### LEG OF LAMB WITH SALSA

1 5 to 6 pound leg of lamb
¼ cup butter or margarine
2 ounces dried small red chiles (pasillas)
2 cloves garlic
¼ cup oil
2 cups (about) pulque or half

water, half tequila (can use beer)
2 onions
8 pickled small green chiles (serranos)
Grated Parmesan cheese

*Pour a little salt in milk when it is fresh; it'll keep much longer.*

Roast lamb on a spit over charcoal or in a smoker grill or in a 325° oven until done as desired, 1½ to 2 hours. Spread thickly with butter and roast 10 to 15 minutes longer, brushing with drippings. Meanwhile, grind dried red chiles and garlic in blender, food grinder or mortar and pestle. Beat in olive oil and liquid to make of thin sauce consistency. Peel and chop onions. Slice lamb and serve sauce over each portion sprinkling with onion and garnishing with a pickled green chile and grated cheese. Makes 8 servings.

The dish is only as good as the sauce. Here are some of my favorite sauces, from Barbecue to Spaghetti:

### BARBECUE SAUCE FOR HAM OR PORK

| | |
|---|---|
| 1 cup sherry | 1 teaspoon garlic powder |
| 1 cup pineapple juice | 1 tablespoon prepared mustard |
| 1 teaspoon ground cloves | ¼ cup apricot jam |
| ¼ cup brown sugar | |

Combine all ingredients and baste ham or pork the last ½ hour of cooking.

### SWEET & SOUR BEER BARBECUE SAUCE

| | |
|---|---|
| 1 cup beer | 2 tablespoons vinegar |
| ½ cup chili sauce | 2 teaspoons sugar |
| 1 cup tomato sauce | 2 tablespoons Worcestershire |
| 2 tablespoons instant minced | sauce |
| onion | 2 teaspoons chili powder |

Combine all the ingredients in a saucepan. Bring to a boil and cook two minutes. Use as a basting sauce for chicken, spareribs or hot dogs.

### TERIYAKI SAUCE

| | |
|---|---|
| 1 tablespoon soy sauce | 2 tablespoons sherry |
| 2 tablespoons sugar | 2 tablespoons oil |
| 4 teaspoons powdered ginger | ½ cup consomme |
| 1 clove garlic, minced | |

*When cutting a pie, dip the knife in cold water.*

Combine all ingredients and use as a marinade. An excellent baste for chicken, beef, turkey and fish.

## SPAGHETTI SAUCE

| | |
|---|---|
| 1 pound ground beef | 2 cups beef stock or bouillon |
| 1 pound ground veal | ½ teaspoon oregano |
| ½ cup olive oil | ½ teaspoon sweet basil |
| 1 large onion, chopped | ¼ teaspoon nutmeg |
| 2 cloves garlic, chopped | ¼ teaspoon rosemary |
| ¾ pound mushrooms, sliced | ½ bay leaf |
| 1 cup Burgundy | ½ teaspoon paprika |
| 1 #2 can solid pack tomatoes | 1 teaspoon salt |
| (or 2 pounds fresh tomatoes) | ½ teaspoon freshly ground |
| 1 #1 can tomato puree | black pepper |

Add meat to a pan and place in a moderate 350° oven; let stay a few minutes, stirring a few times so that it will brown evenly. Heat the olive oil in a kettle, add onion, garlic and mushrooms. Cook and stir 5 minutes; add Burgundy, tomatoes, tomato puree and beef stock or bouillon. Let cook gently 10 minutes; add the meat. Add spices. Let simmer 1½ hours, skimming occasionally.

This makes a delicious, tangy sauce to serve over hot boiled spaghetti, or as an all purpose sauce for meat loaf, for baking fish and for chicken cacciatore.

## ANCHOVY SAUCE

| | |
|---|---|
| ⅓ cup olive oil | ½ cup parsley, finely chopped |
| Oil remaining in one 2-ounce can | 1 2-ounce can anchovy fillets |
| of anchovy fillets | Pinch basil |
| 2 tablespoons butter | Freshly ground black pepper |
| 4 cloves garlic, minced | |

Warm olive oil and anchovy oil in a saucepan; add butter and simmer until melted. Add garlic and parsley, sauté 4 minutes over low heat. Add anchovy fillets, basil and ground pepper; continue cooking until

*Save syrup from canned fruits to use as toppings for ice cream or cake.*

sauce is thoroughly heated and the anchovies have blended into the sauce. Stir occasionally. Serves 4. Great with any pasta or poached fish.

## MUSHROOM SAUCE

¼ cup olive oil
¼ cup butter
1 clove garlic, minced
1 pound mushrooms, sliced thin

½ teaspoon salt
¼ teaspoon oregano
Freshly ground black pepper

Warm olive oil in a saucepan; add butter and simmer until melted. Add garlic, mushrooms and salt and cook until mushrooms are tender (about 12 minutes), stirring constantly. Add oregano and pepper; mix thoroughly. Serves 4. Beautiful on pasta; but lovely on veal cutlets or steak.

## CHICKEN LIVER SAUCE

¼ cup olive oil
2 tablespoons butter
1 cup onion, finely chopped
1 small green pepper, finely chopped
2 chicken (or 1 turkey) gizzards, finely chopped
6 chicken livers, finely chopped
4 strips raw bacon, finely chopped

4 cloves garlic, finely chopped
3 tablespoons parsley, finely chopped
½ teaspoon salt
Freshly ground black pepper
4 small fresh tomatoes, peeled and diced
Pinch dry crushed red pepper

Warm olive oil in a saucepan; add butter and simmer until melted. Add onion, green pepper; sauté until almost tender. Put gizzards in pot; cook slowly 20 minutes. Add chicken livers, bacon, garlic, parsley, salt, black and red pepper. Cook over low heat for 10 minutes. Put in tomatoes and bring to boiling point. Cover and cook over low heat 20 minutes, stirring occasionally. Serves 4.

*To make stained bottles beautifully clean and bright, pour in salt and cover with vinegar. Let stand a few hours and shake. Good for vases and lamp bases.*

## CLAM SAUCE

¼ cup olive oil  
½ cup butter  
6 cloves garlic, finely chopped  
¼ cup parsley, finely chopped  
1 tablespoon basillico  
  (sweet basil)  
3 tablespoons Parmesan cheese,  
  grated  

Pinch dry crushed red pepper  
Freshly ground black pepper  
10-12 large cherrystone clams,  
  chopped coarsely, or 1 can  
  minced clams  

Warm olive oil in a saucepan; add butter and simmer until melted. Add garlic, parsley, basillico, Parmesan cheese, red and black pepper. Bring to a boiling point. Add clams with their natural liquid and again bring to a boiling point. Serve over spaghetti, noodles or linguini. To make red clam sauce, add 1 cup tomato sauce when adding clams. Serves 4.

*Leftover sausage meat is wonderful when added to your pancake batter, or mix it with leftover mashed potatoes, form in patties and brown in butter.*

# Poultry

# The Words about Poultry

Say "poultry" and the first word that comes to your mind is "chicken." Again let us hear from Dr. Dichter. "Chickening out" is symbolic of the bird's assumed cowardice, says the perceptive doctor. The cock, on the other hand, is a symbol of virility and symbolizing ressurection, appears on many medieval churches and buildings. I don't have to tell you that chicken is prepared in many different national ways. Each region seems to have a method and a recipe—southern fried chicken, Tennessee fried chicken, Kentucky fried chicken, Maryland fried chicken. Throughout the world, too, chicken has its own way —Chicken paprikash from Hungary, chicken sauté chasseur, chicken hunter style and smothered chicken. The different recipes are an indication, says Dr. Dichter, of how universally man's monotonous fare of just plain chicken has resulted in culinary inventions of infinite variety. The development of exotic chicken dishes seems to offer a culinary challenge. But Dichter hastens to point out the fact that the chicken is considered to be far less masculine than steak. It has elements of lightness and thus can be fed to sick people as well as to chickens. Hyman Goldberg (we used to call her—or him—Prudence Penny) tells about a lady who lived in the Bronx and kept two chickens on the balcony of her apartment. One chicken became ill. So she killed the healthy one to make a broth to feed the sick one. This should prove some sort of a point. I am passing on my own suggestions of what to do with these stupid birds—along with the turkey—knowing full well that these could hardly be the birds discussed as "the birds and the bees."

65

## CHICKEN IN CHERRIES JUBILEE

| | |
|---|---|
| 6 to 8 chicken breasts | 1 cup chicken broth |
| ½ cup flour | ½ cup dry vermouth |
| 1 teaspoon salt | 2 cups pitted Bing cherries, |
| ½ teaspoon pepper | drained |
| 1 teaspoon paprika | 8 segments of orange |
| 2 tablespoons butter or | ½ cup brandy |
| margarine | ¼ cup cherry juice |
| 2 tablespoons oil | |

Dust the chicken breasts with the flour, salt, pepper and paprika. Brown slowly in the oil and butter. When chicken is nicely browned, add the broth and vermouth. Cover and simmer in 350° oven until the chicken is done and tender—about 20 minutes. Remove cover and add the fruits. Add the brandy, allow to heat through and set aflame. When brandy stops burning, blend in the cherry juice and serve. Serves 6-8.


## CHICKEN-ASPARAGUS

| | |
|---|---|
| 3 complete chicken breasts, | 1 3-ounce package cream |
| boned | cheese, diced |
| ¼ cup flour | 18 asparagus stalks, cooked |
| 2 eggs, beaten | 1 cup sour cream |
| Salt and pepper | ⅓ cup grated Parmesan cheese |
| ½ cup butter or margarine | |

Have the butcher bone the chicken breasts. Cut in half. Pound them out flat. Dip each into flour and then into beaten egg. Season with salt and pepper. Fry in butter or margarine until golden and cooked through— about 20 minutes. Arrange in heat-proof shallow dish. Cover with diced cream cheese. Place 3 asparagus tips on each. Top with sour cream and sprinkle with grated Parmesan cheese. Place under broiler about 4-5 inches from the flame and cook until cheese browns, about 3-5 minutes. Watch closely. Makes 6 servings.

---

*The garlic press, lemon squeezer, egg beater or grater should be held in running water immediately after use. It keeps them from rusting or tarnishing.*

66

## BREAST OF CHICKEN FLAMBÉ

4 chicken breasts (or allow 1 per serving)
Flour, salt, pepper, paprika
2 tablespoons oil
2 tablespoons butter
¼ cup brandy
2 tablespoons chopped onion (shallot)
2 cups corn bread stuffing (½ cup per serving)
2 tablespoons chopped parsley
½ cup dry vermouth
4 pieces aluminum foil, 6 inches square
4 slices boiled ham (prosciutto if possible, and 1 slice to a serving), 4 inches square
½ cup white sauce (can use canned)
½ cup Hollandaise sauce (can use canned)

Dust the chicken breasts with flour, salt, pepper and paprika. (Don't dredge the chicken, just sprinkle it lightly). Heat one half of the oil and butter and brown chicken breasts. Drain off fat. Add brandy and when it is hot, touch a match to it. Let flame die out. Sauté onion in remaining oil and butter until golden and transparent. Add to dressing along with parsley. Moisten dressing with vermouth and enough of the sauce in the chicken pan to bring the dressing to the proper consistency. Butter the aluminum sheets. Place a serving of dressing on each sheet. Top with ham, then with chicken. Combine the two sauces and top the chicken with it. Fold up the sides of the foil to contain the sauce. Place on a cookie sheet or low-lip baking dish and finish in a 400° oven or until the dish is thoroughly heated through.

## CHICKEN WITH LEMON

1 2½-3 pound broiler, fryer, cut up
1 teaspoon monosodium glutamate
1 teaspoon salt
¼ cup butter or margarine
1 tablespoon lemon juice
1 teaspoon grated lemon peel
2 teaspoons sugar
½ cup light cream
2 tablespoons grated Parmesan cheese
1 lemon, thinly sliced

*To keep cauliflower snowy white, soak for a half hour in cold salt water before cooking.*

Sprinkle chicken with monosodium glutamate and salt. Brown in butter on both sides. Cover and simmer 30 minutes or until tender. Remove chicken. Stir lemon juice and peel and sugar into pan drippings. Slowly add cream and bring to a boil. Return chicken to skillet, heat a few minutes. Arrange chicken on heat-proof serving dish. Pour on sauce, sprinkle with Parmesan cheese. Top with sliced lemon and dot with butter. Brown under broiler. Makes 4 servings.

### ROAST CHICKEN IN SOUR CREAM

1 5-pound roasting chicken, cut into pieces
½ cup all-purpose flour
Salt and pepper to taste
¾ cup olive oil
¾ cup butter
¼ cup broth

½ pound mushrooms
1 small onion, minced
1 small clove garlic, minced
2 teaspoons flour
½ cup heavy sweet cream
½ cup sour cream

Simmer giblets in water to cover, adding more as it cooks away, to make one-fourth cup rich broth. Wash chicken thoroughly; dry well. Shake pieces in a paper bag containing flour well seasoned with salt and pepper. Pour oil into large heavy-bottomed skillet; heat; add chicken, turning pieces to brown on both sides. Meanwhile butter roasting pan generously. When the chicken has browned, remove and arrange pieces in roasting pan, dot each with butter, using all but two tablespoons. Pour giblet broth over, cover pan tightly and bake in moderate oven, 350°, until chicken is tender—about 45 minutes.

Shortly before serving, melt two tablespoons of butter in a pan; add the washed mushrooms—large ones cut into quarters, minced onion and garlic; cover and let cook until mushrooms are tender—about 10 minutes. Stir in flour, add both sweet and sour cream, salt and pepper to taste, and heat slowly, stirring constantly, almost to the boiling point. Place hot chicken on hot platter, pour piping hot sauce over and serve immediately. Makes 6 servings.

*Put a piece of apple in your brown sugar jar to keep it from drying out and lumping.*

## THE TURKEY

Select a fresh, plump turkey allowing about one pound for each serving. If you are using a frozen turkey, try to allow it to thaw about four days in the plastic container in the refrigerator. It will thaw overnight at room temperature. If you are stuck with a real emergency, run tap water over the turkey in the container. The neck is usually found in the body cavity and a package of giblets usually under the neck flap. Put these in a 3 quart sauce pan. The idea of this is that each time we season the dressing, we will add some of the seasoning to the giblets and neck from which we will make a stock for our gravy. With half of a lemon rub the inside of the bird thoroughly and sprinkle with salt, pepper and monosodium glutamate.

Now, we start the dressing. We will allow about a cup of dressing for each pound of weight on the turkey. The recipe ingredients are for a fourteen pound bird and you may increase or decrease the following:

8 cups stale toasted bread cubes about half-inch square
3 cups corn bread, diced and crumbled
¾ pound butter
2 cups onion, chopped
1 cup celery, chopped
½ cup parsley, chopped
2 cloves garlic, chopped
1 tablespoon Worcestershire
2 tablespoons herbs (for those of you who are old-fashioned sage and savory lovers . . . have at it. For myself, I prefer a mixture of thyme, sweet basil and rosemary).
2 cups fruit (I vary this, using the diced fruit such as apricots, prunes and apples one time, and pineapple and mandarin orange sections another time).
1 cup chopped salted nuts (pine nuts, walnuts, almonds, pecans or a mixture)
¼ cup brandy
½ cup or more, dry vermouth

Using one-half pound butter, sauté the onions, celery and garlic until they are soft and transparent, but not brown. Put three tablespoons of the vegetable mixture with the giblets . . . add the rest to the bread crumbs. Add the balance of the ingredients, remembering to add a small amount of each to the gravy stock. When the wine has been

---

*Run your stale dried up cheese through your meat grinder with a little raw onion—a great spread or dip base.*

added, the dressing should be tossed lightly. It should be reasonably dry, and if your taste indicates a moist dressing, add water or stock. (I have never used eggs in this dressing recipe, feeling that it would not need it.) Stuff the bird loosely with the dressing fore and aft. Secure with skewers. Rub the skin of the bird with the remaining one-quarter pound of butter. Place the bird *breast down* in a rack in an open pan in a 275° oven allowing twenty-two minutes to a pound. Double check by inserting a meat thermometer at the point where the thigh meets the body and bring this internal meat temperature up to about 180°. Allow enough time so that the turkey is done one-half hour before serving time. When the bird is taken from the oven, place it on its back on a warm platter and allow it to set up for about one-half hour for ease of carving, saving the juices for the gravy making. The giblets should be covered with water and slowly simmered for an hour and one-half. The stock should be strained. The giblets may be finely chopped and included with the gravy if so desired.

### GRAVY

If there is any fat among the drippings, measure off about one-fourth of a cup and melt in a heavy pot. Add 1/8 cup flour and 1/8 cup cornstarch and cook into the fat. If there are any more crusty drippings in the bottom of the pan, add them at this time. Slowly stir in the stock, bring to a boil, adjust for salt and pepper, seasoning to taste. Add one tablespoon of tomato paste, ¼ cup of currant jelly and again adjust seasonings. If a thicker gravy is desired, mix 2 tablespoons cornstarch and ½ cup water together and add, stirring constantly until the proper degree of thickness is reached.

### TURKEY ENCHILADA

1 4-ounce can green chiles
2 tablespoons oil
1 large onion, chopped
1 clove garlic, minced
2 8-ounce cans tomato sauce
1 teaspoon oregano
1 teaspoon salt

3 cups ground cooked turkey
2 cups shredded Jack or
   mozzarella cheese
2 2¼-ounce cans sliced ripe
   olives
1½ cups cottage cheese
12 corn tortillas

*To keep cheese fresh and free from mold, place in a plastic bag with a fourth teaspoon vinegar. Store in refrigerator.*

Remove seeds from chiles and chop the chiles fine. Heat oil, add chiles, onion and garlic and cook until onion is tender but not browned. Add tomato sauce, oregano and salt. Simmer about 5 minutes. Meanwhile, combine turkey, 1½ cups Jack cheese, olives and cottage cheese. Dip tortillas one by one in simmering sauce until limp, then fill with the turkey mixture. Roll up and place seam side down in a shallow baking dish. Pour sauce over enchiladas and sprinkle with remaining cheese. Bake at 350° for 25 minutes, until heated through and bubbly. Makes 6 servings.

### ROAST DUCK WITH ORANGES

| | |
|---|---|
| 2 ducklings, each 4 to 5 pounds ready-to-cook weight | 1½ tablespoons lemon juice |
| Salt | 3 teaspoons arrowroot starch |
| 3 medium oranges | ½ cup sweet sherry |
| 2 tablespoons sugar | ⅓ cup Grand Marnier or Triple Sec |
| 2 teaspoons vinegar | |
| 2 cups thick veal stock or canned condensed beef broth | |

Clean ducklings and pat dry. Rub inside of ducks with salt; skewer opening and lace shut. Prick skin well all over to allow fat to escape. Roast on a rack in shallow pan in hot oven (400°) about 1½ hours or till meaty part of leg feels tender when pressed (use paper towel). Spoon off fat occasionally. While ducks roast, shave peel from 2 of the oranges with vegetable parer and cut in julienne strips; squeeze juice from all 3 oranges. Set peel and juice aside. When ducks are done, place on heated platter and keep hot while making Orange Sauce.

TO MAKE ORANGE SAUCE: Remove drippings from roasting pan and skim off fat; set pan juices aside. Caramelize the sugar with vinegar in roasting pan; add reserved pan juices, veal stock, orange juice and peel, and lemon juice. Cook sauce rapidly to reduce by half. Blend arrowroot and sherry; gradually stir into sauce; cook, stirring, 6 to 8 minutes or till thick and clear—don't let bubble. Add Grand Marnier just before serving.

*Add salt to a crisp green salad just before serving, otherwise the salt may wilt the greens.*

To serve, garnish ducklings with orange sections, if desired. Pass hot Orange Sauce. Makes 8 servings.

## CORNISH HENS

6 Cornish hens (1 for each person
2 teaspoons salt
¼ teaspoon white pepper
½ teaspoon nutmeg
2 tablespoons lemon juice
1 clove garlic, minced

½ cup butter
1 cup orange juice, or ½ cup orange juice and ½ cup white wine
2 cups Orange Sauce
Orange slices and parsley

Dry hens with paper toweling. Combine salt, pepper, nutmeg, lemon juice and garlic and rub well into skin of hens; place them in shallow baking pan with ends of legs tied together. Pour butter over hens and place in 350° oven to roast for 15 minutes. Pour orange juice (or combination orange juice and wine) over hens; roast 45 minutes additional, basting frequently with pan juices, until hens are tender. The leg meat will be soft and the hens golden brown. Remove from pan and keep warm on hot platter while preparing Orange Sauce; then pour half the sauce over hens and garnish with orange slices and parsley. Serve remaining sauce separately. Serves 6.

## ORANGE COINTREAU SAUCE

2 cups liquid (pan drippings plus sufficient orange juice)
2 tablespoons butter
2 tablespoons flour

2 tablespoons Cointreau or orange Curaçao
2 oranges cut into ½-inch slices (optional)

Pour pan drippings from roaster and add sufficient orange juice to make 2 cups liquid. Melt butter in saucepan; add flour and stir until smooth and bubbly. Add orange juice mixture slowly, stirring until heated and blended. Stir in Cointreau and orange slices; simmer 5 minutes. Adjust seasonings, adding salt if necessary and ⅛ teaspoon nutmeg, if desired.

*A little salt in coffee that has cooked too long will take out the bitter taste.*

## ROAST GOOSE

| | |
|---|---|
| 1 8-10 pound goose | Salt and freshly-ground black |
| Flour | pepper |
| | Dry bread crumbs |

Stuff and tie goose and sprinkle lightly with seasoned flour. Roast in a hot oven (425°) for 15 minutes; reduce heat to 350° and continue roasting until goose is tender (about 25 minutes per pound if stuffed). Do not baste goose during cooking time as it is already fat enough. Remove fat several times during cooking. It will keep indefinitely in a cool place. 15 minutes before end of cooking time, sprinkle bird lightly with dry bread crumbs; raise oven heat to 425° and cook for final 15 minutes.

### Stuffing for Goose

| | |
|---|---|
| 1 large onion, finely chopped | Juice of ½ lemon |
| Lard | Thyme and marjoram |
| ½ pound sausage meat | Salt and freshly-ground black |
| 4 tablespoons finely chopped | pepper |
| parsley | ½ pound poultry livers, |
| 4 anchovy fillets, finely | chopped |
| chopped | ½ cup dry bread crumbs |
| 2 eggs | |

Sauté finely chopped onion in lard until transparent. Add sausage meat and sauté with onion until golden. Combine onion and sausage mixture in a bowl with finely chopped parsley and anchovy fillets, eggs, lemon juice, thyme, marjoram, salt and black pepper, to taste. Sauté chopped poultry livers in remaining fat; add bread crumbs and toss until golden. Combine with other ingredients and stuff bird loosely.

*Always rub the insides of chicken and other fowl with lemon juice. This tenderizes as well as sweetens.*

# Seafoods

# The Words about Seafoods

Since the beginning of time, man has battled the sea for food. The fortunes of the fishing fleet have determined the fortunes of the people of the fishing nations. The sea has carried hopes and fears. Poets have loved it and hardened sailors cursed it, yet to return again and again. There is a connection between the sea and religion. Moses cautioned his people about shellfish and forbade the eating of them in his dietary laws. Jesus used the parable of the casting of the net to demonstrate the good and bad in all of us. When he spoke on that mystic day on the mountainside he divided the few fish to feed the multitude. There is a great roll call: clams, crabs, oysters, shrimp, lobster, scallops, abalone and on and on through bass and trout and sole. Properly prepared there is no counting the blessings the sea furnishes our tables. This is not an extensive section, but it contains a few of my best seafood offerings.

77

### SOLE STUFFED WITH SHRIMP

2 shallots
2 tablespoons slivered almonds
12 shrimp (cooked)
8 mushroom stems

2 cups Mornay sauce
6 sole (flounder) fillets
Salt and pepper
Bread crumbs

Chop shallots fine. Sauté them and the slivered almonds in a little butter. Grind the shrimp and mushroom stems and add to the shallots. Cook, stirring, for several minutes. Take off fire and bind with two tablespoons Mornay sauce. Spread flounder fillets with this mixture, salt and pepper, then roll up fillets and secure with toothpick. Arrange fillets in a buttered ovenproof dish. Now pour over them the rest of the Mornay sauce. Sprinkle a few bread crumbs over all, place in 350° pre-heated oven for twenty minutes—or until browned. Serves 4.

*Mornay Sauce*:

2 tablespoons flour
2 tablespoons butter
¾ cup clear chicken stock
¼ cup Chablis

1 cup light cream
2 tablespoons freshly grated
Swiss cheese

In double boiler, blend flour and butter. Add slowly, stirring, chicken stock, Chablis, and light cream. Cook to thicken slightly. Add cheese and stir until melted.

### FILLET OF SOLE, BONNE FEMME

⅓ cup butter
2 shallots, chopped
Pinch chopped parsley
¼ cup sliced mushrooms
4 fillets of sole

Salt and pepper
½ cup white wine
¼ pint fish broth
2 tablespoons flour

Butter the bottom of a baking dish and sprinkle with the shallots, parsley and mushrooms. Lay the sole upon this garnish. Salt, pepper and moisten with the white wine and fish broth. Poach gently, and baste occasionally. Drain off the cooking liquor into a sauce pan and

*Soak fish in strong salt water for a short time before cooking. This removes the muddy taste that so often accompanies fish.*

reduce to half its volume in cooking. Add paste made from flour and butter. Pour over the sole and set to glaze in very hot oven. Serves 4.

### CHEESE STUFFED FISH FILLETS

| | |
|---|---|
| 2 pounds fish fillets | Cheese stuffing |
| 1 teaspoon salt | 2 tablespoons melted butter |
| Dash pepper | Paprika |

Sprinkle fish with salt and pepper. Place half the fillets, skin side down. in a well greased baking dish. Place stuffing on fish and cover with remaining fillets. Brush fish with butter and sprinkle with paprika. Bake in 350° oven for 30 to 35 minutes or until fish flakes easily with fork. Makes 6 servings.

*Cheese Stuffing:*

| | |
|---|---|
| 1 cup minced onion | 2 tablespoons minced parsley |
| ¼ cup shortening | 2 teaspoons dry mustard |
| 2 cups toasted bread cubes | ½ teaspoon salt |
| 1 cup shredded Cheddar cheese | Pepper to taste |

Sauté onion in shortening until tender. Add bread cubes, cheese, parsley, mustard, salt and pepper. Mix thoroughly.

### MAHI MAHI IN GRAPE SAUCE

| | |
|---|---|
| 1 pound mahi mahi fillets | 1 cup seedless grapes or 1 can |
| ⅓ cup flour | (about 9 oz.) seedless |
| 1 teaspoon salt | grapes, drained |
| ½ teaspoon pepper | ½ cup dry vermouth |
| ½ cube (¼ cup) butter or margarine | |

Cut fillets into serving size pieces; dust with flour seasoned with salt and pepper. In a frying pan, melt butter; brown fish lightly on both sides. Add grapes and vermouth. Cover and simmer 3 minutes. Makes 4 servings.

---

*Sausages will not shrink and shrivel if you boil them about ten minutes before you fry them.*

## ASPARAGUS SALMON

2 pounds fresh asparagus
1 can (10½-ounce) cream of
   mushroom soup
½ cup milk
1 can (4 ounce) mushrooms,
   drained
1 tablespoon butter or
   margarine

4 salmon steaks
¼ cup butter or margarine
½ teaspoon basil
1 tablespoon lemon juice
Paprika

Wash the asparagus thoroughly. Break off each stalk as far down as it snaps easily. Leave stalks whole and cook, covered, in 1-inch of boiling, salted water for 8-10 minutes, or until stalks can be pierced easily with a fork. While the asparagus is cooking, place undiluted soup in saucepan, add milk and heat thoroughly. Sauté mushrooms in 1 tablespoon butter and add to the soup. Broil the salmon steaks on both sides, brushing with mixture of 4 tablespoons butter, basil and lemon juice. Garnish with paprika. Serve immediately with hot asparagus and mushroom sauce. Makes 4 servings.

## PINEAPPLE SHRIMP

1 cup fresh or canned
   pineapple juice
1 cup fresh or canned
   pineapple chunks
½ cup vinegar
1 can tomato sauce (8 ounce)
1 cup sugar
1 cup water
1 teaspoon salt
½ fresh green pepper (cut in
   large pieces)
½ small onion, cut in large
   pieces

1 cup flour
½ teaspoon sugar
½ teaspoon salt
1 egg
1 cup ice water
2 pounds fresh shrimp
2 cups peanut oil
   or salad oil
2 tablespoons cornstarch
½ cup water

---

*To substitute cocoa for chocolate in a recipe, use three level tablespoons of cocoa and an extra tablespoon of butter for each square or ounce of chocolate.*

Combine the first 9 ingredients in a saucepan, bring to boil and remove from heat. In a bowl, mix flour, ½ teaspoon sugar, salt, egg, ice water to make a smooth batter. Peel shell from shrimp, leaving last section and tail intact. Slit in half lengthwise without removing either end; remove black line. Dry shrimp thoroughly, dip in batter and deep fat fry in the oil. Drain on absorbent paper. Thicken sauce with cornstarch mixed with ½ cup water, bring to boil. Remove from heat and pour over shrimp. Serves 6.

## SHRIMP AND SCALLOPS GRUYERE

¾ cup plus 2 tablespoons butter or margarine
¾ cup flour
3 cups milk
12 ounces Swiss Gruyere cheese
¼ teaspoon garlic powder
3½ teaspoons salt
¼ teaspoon white pepper
¼ teaspoon monosodium glutamate

¼ teaspoon dry mustard
2 teaspoons tomato paste
3 teaspoons lemon juice
1 pound raw scallops
½ pound mushrooms, sliced
1 pound cooked, cleaned shrimp
2 tablespoons diced green pepper

Make a cream sauce in the top of a double boiler with ¾ cup butter, the flour and milk. Cut the cheese into small pieces and add to the sauce. Cook and stir until cheese melts. Add garlic powder, 3 teaspoons salt, pepper, monosodium glutamate, mustard, tomato paste and 2 teaspoons lemon juice. Poach scallops for about ten minutes in water to which you have added the remaining lemon juice and salt. Add ½ cup of the broth to the cream sauce. Sauté mushrooms in remaining 2 tablespoons butter and add to sauce. Drain scallops and add with the shrimp to the sauce. Heat for ten to fifteen minutes. Garnish top of serving dish with the green pepper which has been sautéed until tender in a little butter. Makes 8-10 servings.

*To clean discolored aluminum pans, fill with water and add a teaspoon of cream of tartar and then boil for ten minutes. Wash the pan in hot soapy water.*

## LOBSTER AND SHRIMP VERMOUTH

2 tablespoons butter
2 tablespoons oil
½ pound cooked shrimp
  (peeled and deveined)

½ pound lobster tails cut in
  bite-size pieces
¼ cup vermouth
Salt and pepper
Juice of 1 lemon

Combine butter and oil and heat in chafing dish. Add seafood and cook about 5 minutes, then add vermouth and salt and pepper and cook 5 minutes longer. Add lemon juice and allow guests to help themselves with toothpicks. Serves 4.


## LOBSTER TART

6 tablespoons butter
3 tablespoons flour
1½ cups cream
4 tablespoons dry vermouth
1 pound cooked lobster meat

2 cups fresh cracker crumbs
1 teaspoon paprika
2 tablespoons freshly grated
  Parmesan cheese
Additional melted butter

In the top of a double boiler melt 6 tablespoons butter, blend in flour, cook a minute, then add cream and vermouth. Cook, stirring constantly till smooth and creamy. Add the lobster meat, and turn into a low ovenproof casserole. Pound enough crisp crackers to make two cups (use ones with a taste—maybe the sesame-seed kind), add the paprika and the Parmesan cheese and enough melted butter to make a cohesive mass. Knead a moment and then flatten it out to a thickness of a quarter inch. Now cut little biscuits about the size of a silver dollar and arrange them in a pattern on top of the lobster. Cook in a 350° oven for 20 or 25 minutes. Serves 4.


## SCALLOPS AU PARMESAN

¼ cup Chablis
1 pound scallops
¼ cup butter

½ teaspoon garlic salt
¼ cup grated Parmesan cheese

*Peel potatoes with a metal sponge (chore girl). It's easier and quicker. Same idea works on turnips and carrots.*

Pour Chablis over scallops and let marinate for 2 hours. Melt butter in chafing dish or skillet; add scallops and wine. Sprinkle with garlic salt and simmer 10 to 15 minutes. Just before serving sprinkle cheese over the dish. Serve hot with toothpicks. Serves 4.

## CHINESE GARLIC LOBSTER

1 pound cooked pork
2 lobsters
Cooking oil
2 tablespoons chopped green
    ginger

2 cloves garlic, minced
2 cups chicken stock
Cornstarch
Soy sauce

Chop cooked pork very fine. Remove meat of lobsters from shell, saving the shells. Cut meat in chunks and cook in oil until red. Combine pork, lobster, ginger and garlic. Put mixture into shells and steam in stock for 30 minutes, basting once or twice. Before serving, thicken juices with cornstarch mixed in cold water. Season with soy sauce. Serves 4.

## CIOPPINO

¼ cup oil
¼ cup butter or margarine
3 cloves garlic, minced
4 large onions, finely chopped
2 green peppers, finely
    chopped
2 1-pound 12-oz. cans
    tomatoes
2 8-ounce cans tomato sauce
2 bay leaves
¼ cup finely chopped parsley
3 whole cloves

1 teaspoon paprika
¼ teaspoon thyme
2 teaspoons salt
¼ teaspoon pepper
½ teaspoon saffron
½ cup boiling water
½ cup sherry
1 cup dry white wine
1 tablespoon grated orange
    peel
3 to 4 pounds assorted fish
    and shell fish

Heat oil and butter. Add garlic, onion and green pepper and cook until tender but not browned. Add tomatoes, tomato sauce, bay leaves.

*When glassware develops nicks on the edges, rub them smooth with fine sandpaper.*

parsley, cloves, paprika, thyme, salt and pepper. Make a tea by adding the saffron to the boiling water and letting it stand 3 minutes. Add to mixture. Simmer about 30 minutes. Add wines and orange peel and simmer 10 minutes longer. Prepare fish and shell fish. Choose firm-fleshed fish, cut in 2-inch pieces, shelled shrimp, scallops, lobster tails, oysters or clams. Add chunks of lobster tails and simmer about 12 minutes. Add uncooked, fish, shrimp, oysters, clams or scallops and simmer about 5 minutes. Makes 12 servings.

*To keep pie crust from getting soggy, brush the sides and bottom with beaten egg white and place in a hot oven about four minutes.*

# Casseroles

# The Words about Casseroles

I've heard a lot of words about casseroles—most of them unprintable. In the restaurant sense of the word, Prosper Montagne in *Larousse Gastronomique* tells us that in French cooking the term denotes a preparation generally made with rice. Here in America a casserole sometimes defines a dish made of two or more elements, the basis of which can be rice, any pasta (macaroni, spaghetti, etc.) in combination with meat or fish plus a sauce or gravy, and often a variety of vegetables. Here in America, too, a casserole is the dish one takes to a church supper; or what one prepares when one's refrigerator is loaded with leftovers and one wants to use up what's there. I know one cook who tried to make a leftover something that was really a leftover. She called it "planned overs." In all truthfulness the only planning that should be done for these things is in throwing them out. I say this not to slander casseroles, for they can be wondrous things. I say it to warn you against dried up, soup-laden messes which are foisted on us occasionally. A casserole is a thing of beauty when it's properly done. I love them when they're fresh and steaming and the true flavors blend in an harmonious melody of taste. I serve them at parties without fear or trepidition. A *paella* will satisfy the most discerning gourmet. I include a large selection of casseroles for the simple reason that you have asked for them. A couple of them are huge for party fare—double or triple without change in flavor. It's almost impossible to make a mistake with any of them. They are full of hidden things.

87

## $10,000 CASSEROLE

½ pound fine noodles
2 to 3 tablespoons shortening
(½ butter, ½ olive oil)
2 cups chopped onion
2 pounds ground chuck
1 4-ounce can mushrooms
1 can cream of chicken soup
1½ cups milk
½ teaspoon salt

¼ teaspoon pepper
¼ cup soy sauce
1 teaspoon Worcestershire
sauce
½ pound grated Cheddar
cheese
¼ pound mixed salted nuts
1 can Chinese chow mein
(crisp) noodles

Cook and drain noodles. Sauté onion in large skillet in shortening until golden. Add meat, cook until browned. Combine mushrooms, soup and milk and add to meat mixture. Blend in spices, soy and Worcestershire. Mix well and heat thoroughly. Butter a 3-quart casserole and spread cooked noodles over bottom. Cover with meat mixture. Top with cheese. Heat well in 350° oven for 15 minutes until cheese bubbles. Remove and top with nuts and crisp noodles. Return to oven for 10 more minutes cooking time. Serves 10.

## HAM AND ASPARAGUS CASSEROLE

4½ pounds baked ham
1 cup butter
1 cup flour
5 cups light cream
3 cups milk
1 cup dry white wine
1 cup chicken broth
⅔ cup grated sharp cheese
1 cup grated Parmesan cheese
Juice of 2 lemons
3 tablespoons grated onion
2 tablespoons prepared
mustard

2 tablespoons minced parsley
5 teaspoons salt
¼ teaspoon powdered
rosemary
¼ teaspoon pepper
2 cups mayonnaise
3 pounds fresh asparagus
(or 4 10-ounce packages
frozen)
1½ pounds spaghettini

*Rutabaga and turnips will not give you cooking odors if you add a teaspoon of sugar to the water.*

Cut baked ham into 1-inch cubes to make 3 quarts. Refrigerate. Melt butter in large pan and blend in flour. Slowly add cream, milk, wine and chicken broth. Cook until thickened, stirring constantly. Add cheeses and lemon juice. Season with onion, mustard, parsley, 1 teaspoon salt, rosemary and pepper. Remove sauce from heat and stir in mayonnaise. Cook asparagus until barely tender with 1 teaspoon salt. (If you use frozen, cook according to package directions, but only until crisp-tender). Also prepare spaghettini according to package directions (in boiling water with 3 teaspoons salt). When spaghettini is tender, drain and rinse well. Mix together the sauce, the spaghettini and the cubed ham. Now, in 2 large shallow casseroles, arrange layers of the spaghettini-ham mixture and layers of asparagus, dividing the asparagus between the two casseroles. Top each with spaghettini-ham mixture. Bake, uncovered, in a moderate oven, 350°, about 30 minutes or until bubbly. Makes about 20 servings.

### HUNGRY MOB CASSEROLE

1 pound of bacon, crispcd and chopped
1 onion, chopped and sautéed in a little of the bacon fat
2 pounds ground chuck, browned
2 pounds spaghetti, cooked
1 can ripe olives, drained (303)

2 cans mushrooms (4-ounce)
1 can peas (303)
2 cans spaghetti sauce (303)
¼ pound grated Parmesan cheese
¼ pound grated Cheddar cheese

Mix all ingredients together, except Cheddar cheese. Top with Cheddar and bake in 350° oven until cheese bubbles. Serves 10.

### LASAGNE

½ pound ground beef
½ pound ground pork
½ pound Italian sausage
2 tablespoons olive oil

1 medium onion, minced
1 clove garlic
1 teaspoon minced parsley
1½ can tomato paste

*If shredded coconut gets dry, sprinkle it on a baking sheet and heat it in a moderate oven, shaking occasionally, to brown even.*

2 cups water
½ teaspoon salt
½ teaspoon pepper
5 quarts water
3 teaspoons salt
1 pound lasagne

1 pound mozzarella cheese, sliced thin
1 cup ripe olives, halved
¾ pound ricotta
2 tablespoons grated Romano cheese

Brown beef, pork and sausage in saucepan with oil, onion, garlic and parsley. Add tomato paste, 2 cups water and salt and pepper and simmer 1½ hours. Bring 5 quarts of water to a boil, add salt and lasagne (cut in half) and cook 20 minutes, or until tender, stirring almost constantly to prevent sticking together. Drain. Arrange lasagne in casserole in layers, alternating with layers of meat sauce, mozzarella, olives and ricotta, until lasagne is all used, and ending in like sequence, ricotta last. Sprinkle with grated cheese. Bake in moderate oven, 375°, about 20 minutes, or until mozzarella is melted, and serve. Makes 6-8 servings.

### NEAPOLITAN BEAN CASSEROLE

2 pounds dried white marrow beans
Water to cover
1½ pounds ground beef
1 pound ground veal
½ pound ground pork
3 cups fresh bread crumbs
¾ cup milk
2 cups finely chopped onion
2 tablespoons butter
1 cup chopped mushrooms
2 2-ounce tins anchovy fillets, drained and minced
2 cloves garlic, crushed
1 teaspoon salt
½ teaspoon oregano
¼ teaspoon allspice

2 1-pound 14-ounce cans Italian tomatoes
2 cups canned tomato sauce
4 cloves garlic, crushed
2 tablespoons sugar
1 tablespoon minced parsley
1 beef bouillon cube
2 teaspoons salt
1 teaspoon oregano
½ teaspoon pepper
¼ cup Chianti
2 quarts water
2½ cups undiluted canned consomme
Flour
1 cup butter

*No tears in your eyes when you peel onions if you'll hold them under cold running water as you work.*

Cover beans with water and soak overnight. Mix together the beef, veal and pork. Soak bread crumbs in milk and add to the meat along with chopped onions, which have been sautéed in butter until golden, add mushrooms and anchovy fillets. Season with 2 cloves crushed garlic, 1 teaspoon salt, ½ teaspoon oregano and allspice. Mix all together well and shape into balls the size of walnuts (makes about 75). Refrigerate. Heat Italian tomatoes, tomato sauce, 2 cloves crushed garlic, sugar, parsley, beef bouillon cube, 2 teaspoons salt, 1 teaspoon oregano, pepper and Chianti together over medium heat. Simmer gently, breaking up tomatoes with a fork, until flavors blend, about ½ hour. Drain beans, place them in a large kettle, add 2 quarts water and undiluted canned consomme, cover and cook over medium heat until beans are just tender. Set aside. To make casseroles, lightly flour meat balls and brown in a large skillet in 1 cup butter. Drain on paper toweling. Combine meat balls, sauce and beans, divide mixture in half, place in 2 large shallow casseroles. Cover each loosely with aluminum foil and bake in a moderate oven, 350°, for 1 hour. Makes about 15 servings.

## GREEN BEAN AND MUSHROOM CASSEROLE

| | |
|---|---|
| 1 pound green beans, cut in 1-inch pieces | ¼ teaspoon pepper |
| ¼ cup chopped cashew nuts | 1¼ cups milk |
| ¼ cup butter or margarine | ¼ cup sherry |
| ½ pound mushrooms, sliced | 1 tablespoon instant minced onion |
| 3 tablespoons flour | 3 tablespoons grated Parmesan cheese |
| 1 teaspoon seasoned salt | |
| ¼ teaspoon salt | |

Cook and drain beans. Cook nuts in butter 5 minutes; remove nuts. Add mushrooms to remaining butter and cook until lightly browned. Blend in flour and seasonings. Add milk and sherry and cook, stirring, until thickened. Add beans, half the nuts and onion. Mix well and pour into shallow casserole. Sprinkle with remaining nuts and the cheese. Bake in moderate oven, 350°, about 20 minutes. Serves 6.

*Salad greens should be washed and thoroughly dried and then stored in a clean towel or a plastic bag. Never try to crisp them wet.*

## COUNTRY NOODLE CASSEROLE

½ pound sliced bacon
1 package (1 pound) very fine
  egg noodles
  or vermicelli noodles
3 cups cottage cheese
3 cups sour cream
2 cloves garlic, crushed
2 onions, minced
2 tablespoons Worcestershire
  sauce

Dash liquid hot pepper
  seasoning
2 teaspoons salt
1 tablespoon prepared
  horseradish
1 cup grated Parmesan cheese
Extra sour cream, if you like

Fry bacon until crisp. Drain on paper towels and crumble. Cook noodles in boiling salted water until just tender, according to package directions. Drain well. Mix all remaining ingredients, except Parmesan cheese and extra sour cream, in a large bowl. Add noodles and bacon and toss with two forks until well mixed. Turn into a deep 3½-quart buttered casserole. Cover and bake in a moderate oven, 350°, for 30-40 minutes or until heated through. Remove cover, sprinkle surface with ¼ cup Parmesan cheese, broil until golden. Serve remaining Parmesan to sprinkle over each portion, and extra sour cream if you wish. Makes 12 servings.

## PORK CASSEROLE ITALIAN

2 tablespoons salad oil
1 pound boneless pork loin,
  cut in 1-inch strips
½ cup chopped onion
½ cup chopped celery
1 medium green pepper,
  cut into strips
1 can (3 ounce) sliced
  mushrooms, undrained
1 teaspoon Worcestershire
  sauce

1 teaspoon salt
⅛ teaspoon pepper
½ teaspoon dried basil leaves
1 can (10½ oz.) condensed
  cream of mushroom soup,
  undiluted
¼ cup milk
¼ cup dry vermouth
1 8-ounce package spaghetti
1 tomato, peeled and thinly
  sliced

*Beets can be skinned easily if you dip them in cold water right after they finish boiling.*

92

| 1½ cups croutons | 1 cup grated sharp Cheddar |
| 2 tablespoons melted butter | cheese |

In hot oil, in a large skillet, brown the pork strips well. Add onion, celery and green pepper, sauté them until tender. Mix in sliced mushrooms and all the seasonings; simmer, covered, for 25 minutes. Blend in the soup, milk and vermouth; simmer, covered, 5 minutes. Meanwhile, preheat oven to 350°. In 3 quarts boiling, salted water, boil spaghetti, uncovered, for 8 minutes. Drain. In an ungreased 2-quart casserole, combine pork mixture with the drained spaghetti. Overlap the tomato slices around edge of casserole. Toss the croutons with melted butter; sprinkle over tomatoes. Bake for 20 minutes. Top croutons with cheese; bake 10 minutes, or until cheese melts. Makes 6-8 servings.

### BAKED CHICKEN THERMIDOR

| 1 10-oz. package frozen peas | 2 tablespoons white wine |
| 2 cups cut-up cooked chicken | 1 tablespoon lemon juice |
| 1 cup diced celery | ½ teaspoon salt |
| 1 can (5 oz.) water chestnuts, drained and thinly sliced | ½ cup milk |
| ½ cup toasted sliced almonds | 1 10½-oz. can cream of chicken soup, undiluted |
| 2 tablespoons chopped green pepper | 2 white bread slices, cut into cubes |
| 1 tablespoon grated onion | 1 cup grated sharp Cheddar cheese |
| 2 tablespoons chopped pimiento | |

Cook peas as package label directs; drain. Preheat oven to 375°. In 2-quart casserole, combine peas, chicken, celery, water chestnuts, almonds, green pepper, onion and pimiento. Sprinkle with wine, lemon juice and salt. Toss gently to mix well. In small saucepan, combine milk and soup, stirring until smooth. Bring to boiling, stirring. Add to casserole mixture, combining well. Sprinkle with bread cubes; bake 20 minutes, or until sauce is bubbly and bread cubes are toasted. Sprinkle with cheese; bake 5 minutes, or until cheese is melted. Serves 6-8.

*Leftover egg yolks can be poached until firm, cooled and put through a sieve. Great for salads, appetizers, etc.*

## SEAFOOD TETRAZZINI

1 8-ounce package shell
  macaroni
1 tablespoon butter
1 10-ounce can cream of
  celery soup
½ pound fresh mushrooms,
  sliced
1 cup dairy sour cream
½ cup grated sharp Cheddar
  cheese

2 tablespoons sherry
½ pound cooked shrimp, fresh,
  frozen or canned
½ pound crabmeat, fresh,
  frozen or canned
½ pound lobster, fresh, frozen
  or canned
3 tablespoons slivered almonds
  (approximately)

In the morning prepare casserole for baking. Cook macaroni according to package directions. (Add 1 tablespoon of butter to boiling water to prevent sticking). Drain. Sauté mushrooms in butter. Combine celery soup with mushrooms in pan. Add sour cream, cheese and sherry. If frozen seafood is used, defrost early in the day; separate and remove bone and cartilage. Clean and devein shrimp, and if large, split in half, lengthwise. Grease a 6-cup casserole very well; make 3 layers, using 1/3 macaroni, 1/3 seafood and 1/3 celery soup mixture for each. Sprinkle top with almonds. Place in 350° oven and bake 1 hour. Serves 10.

Use 4 cups diced cooked chicken or turkey instead of seafood. A delicious way to utilize leftovers.

## CHICKEN TETRAZZINI CASSEROLE

1 8-ounce package spaghetti,
  cooked
1 tablespoon salad oil
3 tablespoons butter
½ pound fresh mushrooms,
  sliced
½ cup water
¼ teaspoon salt
¼ teaspoon celery salt

Dash Tabasco
2 tablespoons sherry
1 cup sour cream
2 10-ounce cans cream of
  celery soup
¼ pound Herkimer (Cheddar)
  cheese, diced
2 cups diced, cooked chicken

TOPPING:
2 tablespoons bread crumbs

2 tablespoons butter

*Old eggs are smooth and shiny. Fresh eggs look rough and chalky.*

Cook spaghetti according to package directions; add 1 tablespoon salad oil to water to prevent sticking. Cook tender, but not too soft; rinse in hot water, then drain. Heat butter in large skillet; add mushrooms; sauté 5 minutes. Stir in water, salt, celery salt and Tabasco; add sherry. Blend in sour cream and celery soup; toss with spaghetti, cheese and chicken; turn into well-greased 6-cup casserole. Top with bread crumbs and dot with butter; bake in 350° oven 45 minutes or until well heated and browned. Serves 6.

### CHICKEN-TAMALE PIE

¼ cup butter or margarine
1 medium onion, chopped
1 clove garlic, chopped
4 cups cooked chicken meat, in large pieces
2 to 3 teaspoons chili powder
1 cup sliced pitted ripe olives

½ teaspoon coriander
1 10-ounce can tomato puree
1½ teaspoons salt
½ teaspoon pepper
6 cups chicken broth
2 teaspoons salt
2 cups corn meal

In 1 tablespoon melted butter in large skillet, sauté onion and garlic until tender. Add chicken, chili powder, ripe olives, coriander, tomato puree, 1½ teaspoons salt, pepper and ½ cup chicken broth. Cover; simmer 15 minutes. Bring 5½ cups chicken broth to a boil; add 2 teaspoons salt; slowly stir in corn meal. Add 3 tablespoons butter; cook, stirring constantly, 5 minutes. Heat oven to 300°. Butter 3-quart casserole; line it with half of corn-meal mush. Pour in chicken mixture; cover with rest of mush. Bake 1¼ hours. Makes 6 servings.

### SHELLFISH CASSEROLE

1¼ cups macaroni shells
¼ cup butter or margarine
1 tablespoon finely chopped onion
¼ cup flour
1 teaspoon salt
¼ teaspoon white pepper
1 teaspoon paprika
1 pound shelled crab meat,

lobster or shrimp, or combination
1 package frozen artichoke hearts (can use canned— 9 ounce)
3¼ cups milk, scalded
¼ cup sherry
¼ cup Cheddar cheese, grated

*A little salt imparts a mellow taste to tea and makes cocoa richer.*

Cook macaroni shells according to package directions. Melt butter; sauté onion until transparent but not brown. Add flour, salt, pepper, paprika and allow to simmer a minute. Add seafood and allow to heat through. Add milk gradually. Add sherry and allow mixture to simmer about five minutes, stirring gently. Drain macaroni and combine with drained, cooked artichoke hearts to seafood mixture. Turn into large, buttered casserole. Top with grated cheese and place in 350° oven for 20 minutes or until cheese melts. Serves 4.

### SHRIMP OF THE SEA CASSEROLE

2¼ cups cooked fresh shrimp pieces
1 10-ounce package elbow macaroni
¼ cup butter
1 clove garlic, minced or crushed in a garlic press
½ cup chopped fresh mushrooms
3 tablespoons chopped onion
¼ cup butter
¼ cup flour
½ teaspoon salt
⅛ teaspoon black pepper
½ teaspoon Accent

2 cups milk
4 ounces process Cheddar cheese, shredded
4 ounces sharp Cheddar cheese, shredded
2 ounces mozzarella cheese, shredded
2 tablespoons shredded Parmesan cheese
½ cup cream-style cottage cheese
½ cup thick sour cream
½ cup coarse dry bread crumbs or cracker crumbs, buttered

Prepare shrimp and set aside. Cook macaroni according to package directions and set aside. To prepare shrimp—wash about 1½ pounds shrimp in cold water. Drop into a rapidly boiling mixture of 1 quart water; celery leaves; 2 whole cloves; 1 small onion, sliced; 3 to 4 parsley sprigs and 1 tablespoon salt. Cover and cook until water returns to boiling. Remove from heat and let stand, covered, for 5 minutes. Drain shrimp and cover with cold water to chill. Drain; remove tiny legs, shells and black veins. Drain on absorbent paper. Cut into ½-inch pieces. Heat ¼ cup butter in a skillet. Add garlic, mushrooms and onion and cook until onion is soft. Heat ¼ cup butter in a saucepan

*When you crack a favorite dish or plate, put it in a pan of milk and boil it 45 minutes. Usually the crack disappears.*

over low heat. Blend in a mixture of the flour, salt, pepper and Accent. Heat until mixture bubbles, stirring constantly. Remove from heat. Add milk, gradually, stirring constantly. Return to heat and cook, until sauce thickens, stirring constantly. Cook 1 to 2 minutes longer. Remove from heat; cool slightly. Stir in the Cheddar cheeses, mozzarella and Parmesan until melted. Blend in cottage cheese and sour cream. Mix together the sauce, onion mixture, shrimp and macaroni. Turn into a 2½-quart casserole. Top with buttered crumbs. Heat in a 350° oven about 30 minutes, or until crumbs are golden brown and mixture is bubbly. Serves 8-10.

### PAELLA

| | |
|---|---|
| 2½ pound chicken, cut up | 2 teaspoons salt |
| 1 pound lean pork, cubed | 2 cups long grain rice |
| ½ to ¾ cup Spanish olive oil | 1 quart chicken stock |
| 1 teaspoon paprika | 4 7-ounce lobster tails; or 1 |
| 2 whole garlic cloves | pound large shrimp |
| 2 tablespoons minced parsley | 1 quart mussels or clams, well |
| 1 medium onion, minced | scrubbed |
| 1 pimiento, drained, chopped | 1 cup frozen tiny peas |
| ½ teaspoon saffron | 2 tablespoons Spanish sherry |

Separate backs, wing tips and giblets from more tender pieces of chicken; use these in making chicken stock along with chicken bouillon cubes or powder. If using shrimp also, add shrimp shells to the stock. Cut remaining chicken pieces with poultry shears into small pieces. In a very large skillet, sauté the chicken and pork in ½ cup olive oil until crisply browned, sprinkling with paprika as the pieces cook. Place garlic cloves and ¼ of minced onion in pan as chicken browns; remove chicken and pork to large casserole, set aside the garlic. To pan add parsley, remaining onion and the pimiento and, if necessary, more olive oil; cook until onion is soft. Crush saffron with the browned garlic and salt in a mortar and pestle; stir in a tablespoon of warm water to dissolve, add this to onions in pan. Add the rice, stir to glaze with oil. Slowly add the chicken stock, bring to a boil. Transfer rice and stock to the casserole. Remove undershell of lobster tails; hold

*A few grains of rice in the salt shaker will absorb the moisture and keep the salt dry. Works with sugar too.*

frozen tails under hot water a few moments, then pull flesh partially away from hard upper shell. Cut each tail in half, cutting right through hard shell. Place lobster (or shrimp), scrubbed mussels and peas over rice, stir to distribute ingredients. Place casserole in 350° oven, bake uncovered until liquid is absorbed, about 25 minutes. Sprinkle over the top a tablespoon of olive oil and the sherry, cover the casserole, steam in oven or over very low heat on top of stove for about 5 minutes. Serve from the casserole. Makes 8 servings.

NOTE: 1 can minced clams may be substituted for the mussels or clams in shell.

### WICK FOWLER'S "TWO ALARM" CHILI

This recipe comes from the Chili Appreciation Society International, Los Angeles Chapter.

| | |
|---|---|
| 3 pounds ground beef (The true chili lover will ask his butcher for chili-ground beef) | 1 teaspoon Tabasco sauce |
| | 1 tablespoon oregano |
| | 1 tablespoon cumin |
| | 6 red peppers (about 2 inches long)—optional |
| 1 #2 can tomato sauce | 4 tablespoons chili powder |
| 1 onion, chopped | |
| Chopped garlic to taste | 1 tablespoon paprika |
| 1 teaspoon salt | 2 tablespoons flour |
| 1 teaspoon red pepper | |

Sear meat in skillet with onions and garlic. When meat is thoroughly browned, put in tomato sauce, and add some water. Add all other ingredients. Cover with half an inch of water and stir well. Simmer at least an hour and a half, or longer, stirring regularly. Towards the end, skim the grease and add a couple of tablespoons of flour mixed with warm water to thicken. Serve by itself, or with beans (cooked separately), rice or corn meal mush. Serves 8 to 10.

*Fill the cake pan only half full for best results.*

# Vegetables

# The Words about Vegetables

There are a lot of words about vegetables—most of them bad, as any mother who has tried to tease her bewildering offspring into eating his spinach will tell you. But I like the attitude of the *The Gourmet Cookbook* and magazine. Says this most emphatic authority: "Midway between Beau Brummel, who once ate a pea, and George Bernard Shaw, who couldn't see a filet mignon for the raw carrot under his nose, stands the happy gourmet. For this fortunate fellow, the kitchen garden is a treasure-house of textures and flavors to delight his palate. Because vegetables cost us so little, he endows them lavishly with butter and cream and condiments. He remembers that undercooked vegetables have more color, taste and crispness than the overcooked. He spares the water in the cookpot and makes good use of the casserole where butter, seasonings and one or a half-dozen vegetables mellow and blend in mysterious alchemy. And then the happy gourmet eats his vegetables, and he finds them mighty good eating." Again let us assume the position on the psychic couch and listen to Dr. Dichter talk about us and a couple of vegetables we shall feature prominently in these pages. In seeking to discover and then tell us what we are and why we act as we do and think as we do, the Institute of Motivational Research has, indeed, gone far back into the story of the bean, barley, cheese and asparagus. Beans, they report, have been—like rice—symbols of fertility since ancient times. There is a belief that women should not plant beans, for if they do, they will conceive. This is still believed in many parts of Eastern Europe, Greece and in backyard rural areas of

101

the United States. This symbol of fertility derives from the ability of one bean to produce a whole bean plant with many, many bean pods and countless individual beans. Beans represent a good return. Beans are comparable to potatoes in nutrition. Many diets use beans as an important staple. Pork and beans is almost the equal of meat and potatoes. In some ancient religious systems woman was the dominant sex; man definitely played a subordinate role and fatherhood was not honored or even understood. Conception usually was explained as being due to the wind and the eating of beans, or the accidental swallowing of an insect. As for barley, it was traditionally a giver of strength. Even in ancient times barley water, fumes of barley and similar uses of this grain were known to have powerful effect. The name Demeter, goddess of the fruitful soil, means in literal translation "barley mother." The priestesses in Greek times were put into a trance-like state by laying hemp, laurel and barley on hot charcoal ashes to produce narcotic fumes. Today, we still use barley in the preparation of alcoholic beverages (hic). As for asparagus: Well! Or Wow! Most food has acquired a symbolic and psychological meaning far beyond its actual nutritional value and taste. While a shape or general appearance sometimes makes such a symbolic interpretation easier, it is fairly obvious that people in various cultures will reach for explanations of their eating habits. Asparagus, for instance, because of its peculiar shape, is believed to increase sexual potency. Try it sometime.

## ASPARAGUS

Allow a half-pound for each serving. Look for stalks that are green and tender almost the entire length. The tips should be well-formed and tightly closed. Buy stalks that are as nearly uniform as possible since varying sizes will cook in different times. To prepare, break off each stalk as far down as it will snap easily. Wash it thoroughly to release any sand. If you wish, you may pare each stalk thinly with a vegetable parer. Cook in a large shallow skillet. Lay the stalks flat in skillet. Add about an inch of boiling water and add a teaspoon of salt. Allow until the lower part of the stalks are tender but firm.

### ASPARAGUS AMELIO

4 stalks asparagus, cooked, for    2 tablespoons butter
each portion                       ¼ cup Parmesan cheese

Dry cooked asparagus in paper towels. Arrange in a ramekin or shallow baking dish which has been well buttered. Dot with more butter and place in 400° oven until butter melts and asparagus is heated through—about 15 minutes. Sprinkle with cheese and return to oven until butter just browns and cheese starts to brown. Serve immediately.

### ASPARAGUS IN ONION BUTTER SAUCE

¼ cup butter or margarine        2 pounds asparagus, cooked
1 jar (3½ ounces) cocktail       3 tablespoons chopped walnuts
onions                           Salt to taste

Melt butter in large skillet. Drain cocktail onions, reserving 2 table-spoons of onion liquid. Add liquid to melted butter. Add cooked asparagus, cover and allow to heat through about 5 minutes. Add onions and walnuts and salt. Cover and simmer 5 minutes more.

### ASPARAGUS ORIENTAL

2 pounds asparagus               1 teaspoon monosodium
¼ cup butter                     glutamate
1 teaspoon salt                  1½ teaspoons sugar

*Sharpen your kitchen scissors by cutting a piece of sandpaper once or twice with them.*

103

Slice asparagus diagonally into ⅛-inch slices. Sauté rapidly in butter. Season with salt, monosodium glutamate and sugar. This should be done very fast and the asparagus should be crispy. The whole process should take no longer than four minutes.

### ALISON'S BOSTON BAKED BEANS

2 cups dried large navy beans, soaked overnight
1 medium onion, chopped fine
¼ pound salt pork
4 tablespoons brown sugar
½ cup molasses
½ teaspoon salt
⅛ teaspoon pepper
1 teaspoon dry mustard
Hot water to cover

Cook beans, using water beans were soaked in, until skins split when blown on. In bean pot, layer beans with mixture of remaining ingredients. Cook, covered, at low temperature, approximately 250°, for 5 to 6 hours. Check occasionally and add hot water if necessary—always keeping beans covered. Remove cover during last hour of cooking to allow browning.

### BOSSANOVA BEANS

1 #2½ can pork and beans
1 large can chili beans
1 cup onions, chopped fine
8 slices bacon, diced small
½ cup brown sugar
1 cup catsup or enchilada sauce
2 teaspoon chili powder (you may add more to taste)
1 teaspoon powdered cumin
1 cup grated Monterey Jack cheese

Butter a 2-quart casserole or bean pot. Place a layer of beans on the bottom. Then add small amounts of all the other ingredients, except the cheese. Add another layer of beans and repeat until all the beans are used. Bake uncovered at 500° for 15 minutes. Reduce heat to 375, cover, bake 30 minutes more. Add cheese last 15 minutes of cooking.

*To remove rust from the corners of pans, dip a raw potato in cleaning powder and scour.*

104

## RANCHER'S BEAN POT

2 pounds link sausages, halved
3 onions, chopped
3 tablespoons flour
3 1-pound cans pork and beans
1 8-ounce can tomato sauce

1¼ cups water
½ teaspoon salt
¾ teaspoon thyme
1 small bay leaf, crushed
½ teaspoon basil

Brown sausage in large skillet. Remove from pan; pour off fat, reserving ¼ cup. Cook onions and flour in reserved fat stirring till flour is brown. Add sausages and remaining ingredients; heat to boiling. Turn into 3-quart casserole or bean pot. Bake uncovered at 325° for 2 hours, stirring occasionally. Serves 8 to 10.

## SWEET & SOUR RED CABBAGE

1 head red cabbage, sliced thin
2 onions, sliced
2 unpeeled apples, cored and
    sliced
½ cup red currant jelly
1 bay leaf
Salt

Dash of pepper
¼ pound butter, chicken or
    bacon fat
4 medium-size ham knuckles
¼ cup water
3 ounces vinegar

Mix red cabbage with onions, apples, currant jelly, bay leaf, salt and pepper. Put butter, chicken or bacon fat in heavy casserole with tight-fitting cover; add red cabbage, ham knuckles, ¼ cup water. Bring to a boil and cook slowly 2½ hours. Add vinegar at the last minute; remove bay leaf. Serves 6.

## STRING BEANS WITH SOUR CREAM SAUCE

4 pounds green string beans
Salt
Boiling water to cover

Pinch of soda
Cut chives

Wash and cut off the strings of beans, leaving them whole. Tie them securely in 6 or 8 bundles. Lay them in a large enamel pan and sprinkle

*To get the most efficient use of your freezer, keep it full. If you have unused space, fill it with bread or use milk cartons filled with water.*

105

with salt. Pour over them sufficient actively boiling water to cover. Add soda. Cover the pan and bring to a boil. Remove cover; skim carefully and cook until tender, but not floppy. Drain and place the bundles on a preheated platter and remove the strings, being careful not to disturb the symmetry of the beans. Pour over them the following well-seasoned sour cream sauce, sprinkle with cut chives, and serve at once. Serves 6 to 8 as a main dish.

### SOUR CREAM SAUCE

2 tablespoons butter
2 tablespoons flour
1 cup hot milk
Salt and coarsely ground black
  pepper, to taste

1 heaping tablespoon grated
  onion
1 cup sour cream
1 tablespoon cut chives

In the top of a small enamel double boiler, make a cream sauce with butter, flour and milk. Cook until well thickened and season to taste with salt and pepper. Add the grated onion, stir, and cover; continue cooking over hot water for fifteen minutes. Just before serving, add sour cream and stir constantly until heated through. Be careful not to overheat. Pour over the string beans, sprinkle with chives. Serves 6 to 8.

### GREEK STYLE GREEN BEANS

1½ pounds green beans
¼ cup olive oil
2 or 3 large tomatoes, peeled
  and chopped, or 1-pound
  can tomatoes

1 medium onion, sliced
½ teaspoon sugar
½ teaspoon salt
⅛ teaspoon oregano
Dash of pepper

Beans which are past their prime and becoming just a little tough are fine for this dish. Break in lengths and place in heavy pot with remaining ingredients. Simmer tightly covered until beans are very tender, about 1 hour. Serves 6.

---

*Keep your refrigerator fresh inside by using a weak solution of baking soda and water to wash it down every ten days.*

## EGGPLANT PARMIGIANA

2 cups olive oil
1 clove garlic, minced
1 large onion, chopped
5 cups canned Italian-style
   tomatoes
½ teaspoon basil
Salt and pepper
1 cup flour

2 eggs, beaten
1 cup milk
2 medium eggplant pared and
   cut in ½-inch slices
1 cup grated Parmesan cheese
8 ounces mozzarella cheese,
   diced
¼ cup butter

Heat ¼ cup of the oil in skillet. Sauté garlic and onion in it until soft. Add tomatoes, basil, salt and pepper. Cook, covered, stirring occasionally, 30 minutes. Make batter with flour, eggs and milk. Dip eggplant slices in it and fry in remaining hot oil until just browned on both sides. Add more olive oil after each frying. Arrange alternate layers of eggplant, sauce and cheeses in casserole. Sprinkle each layer with salt and pepper. Dot with butter and bake in 350° oven 30 minutes. Serves 6 to 8.

## POTATO PEANUT BAKE

3 cups grated white potato
½ teaspoon salt
Pepper
1 cup roasted peanuts, crushed
   or ground in food chopper

1 cup grated cheese
2 tablespoons butter
1 cup milk

Place layer of grated potato, which have been salted and peppered, in baking dish, add a layer of crushed peanuts and then a layer of cheese. Dot with butter. Follow this procedure until all ingredients are used. Sprinkle top layer with peanuts and pour milk over mixture. Bake 30 minutes at 350°.

NOTE: As you grate the potatoes, put them in 1½ quarts water and ½ cup lemon juice. This keeps them white until you are ready to assemble the dish.

---

*For an extra flaky upper crust on your pie, brush lightly with cold water or milk.*

## RICE OR BULGUR (CRACKED WHEAT) PILAFF

2 tablespoons butter
2 tablespoons chopped onion
1 clove garlic, minced
2 cups rice, or 2 cups cracked
  wheat

2 tablespoons chopped parsley
½ teaspoon powdered oregano
4 cups chicken stock or light
  stock
¼ cup pine nuts

In a large casserole melt butter and sauté onion and garlic until transparent. Add the rice (or cracked wheat), and stir well. Add the rest of the ingredients except the stock and pine nuts. Sauté 5 minutes, stirring occasionally. Add the stock. Cover the casserole and place in a 350° oven for 1 hour. Just before serving, sprinkle the pine nuts over all.

## ACORN SQUASH AND CARROT BAKE

6 acorn squash
Salt and pepper
Melted butter or margarine
1 pound carrots
¼ teaspoon ground orange peel,

or 1 teaspoon fresh grated
  peel
1 egg
¼ cup brown sugar
¼ teaspoon salt

Wash and cut squash in half. Leave seeds in to keep the flesh moist. Sprinkle with salt, pepper and brush with melted butter. Put the squash on a cookie sheet in a 350° oven until tender, about an hour. Meanwhile, wash and scrape carrots. Cut in chunks. Cook in small amount of salted, boiling water until tender. Remove the seeds from squash and scoop out the cooked flesh. Save 6 shells. Put in electric beating bowl. Add drained cooked carrots, orange peel, egg, brown sugar and salt. Whip until fluffy. Put whipped mixture into six of the squash shells. Dot with butter and brown under broiler. Serves 6.

## STUFFED SQUASH

8 zucchini
½ pound ground round steak
½ cup raw rice
Juice of ½ lemon

1 tablespoon olive oil
1 small onion, diced finely
1 small clove garlic, diced finely
  (optional)

*To get more juice out of lemons quickly heat them in hot water for several minutes before squeezing. Same goes for oranges.*

Few sprigs parsley, chopped fine     ⅛ teaspoon pepper
½ teaspoon salt

Wash zucchini well; cut off about 1 inch of stem end and hollow out the insides and mix thoroughly with remaining ingredients. Then stuff the squash, place in a large pan and cover with water. Place a plate or other pan on top to hold solid and cook over a slow fire thirty minutes. If there is more than enough filling to stuff the squash, make the remainder in small balls and wrap in parboiled young tender grape leaves or cabbage or leaf lettuce. The squash, when left over, makes not only a tasty, but very attractive dish when sliced and served cold.

### TOMATOES PROVENCAL

16 large, perfect, ripe tomatoes
Salt and coarsely ground black
    pepper
10 slices white bread
1 cup consomme
1 2-ounce can anchovy fillets
8 tablespoons olive oil

6 tablespoons raw onion,
    chopped
1 teaspoon coarsely chopped
    garlic
3 heaping tablespoons chopped
    parsley
1 cup toasted bread crumbs
6 tablespoons olive oil

Cut off a slice from the stem end of the tomatoes and scoop out most of the pulp. Save the pulp, but discard as many seeds as possible. Sprinkle the tomatoes inside with salt and coarsely ground black pepper, and turn upside down on a big platter to drain. In the meantime, remove crusts from bread and cut in little cubes. Pour the consomme over the bread cubes. Add 8 of the anchovy fillets to the soaked bread and rub the bread and anchovies through a coarse sieve. Heat 8 tablespoons olive oil in a large heavy iron frying pan, and when very hot place the tomatoes, cut side down, in the pan so that they do not touch each other (it may be necessary to fry only half of them at a time, for they must not be crowded. The purpose of doing this to the emptied tomatoes is so that they will retain their shape), and cook on a low flame for 2 minutes, then turn them over carefully with a spatula or pancake turner and cook for 1 minute longer. Remove from fire and place them side by side in 2 large rectangular glass baking dishes approximately 12″ by 7″ by 1½″ deep, which have been rubbed lightly

---

*To put attractive scalloped edges on thin cucumber slices, run the tines of a fork lengthwise over the cucumber before you slice it.*

with a little olive oil, cut side up. Place 6 tablespoons olive oil in a small frying pan and slowly cook the onion until it starts to brown lightly; then add the coarsely chopped tomato pulp, garlic, 2 tablespoons of the chopped parsley, and season to taste with salt and coarsely ground black pepper. Cook slowly for 3 minutes, then remove from fire and add the puree of soaked bread and anchovies. Mix well and stuff the tomatoes. Sprinkle them liberally with toasted bread crumbs and trickle a little olive oil over each. Place in 450° oven and bake until browned or for about 12-15 minutes. Sprinkle with remaining chopped parsley and serve. Serves 6 to 8.

### FRIED TOMATOES WITH CREAM GRAVY

| | |
|---|---|
| 8 firm tomatoes | 4 tablespoons butter |
| Salt and pepper | 4 tablespoons bacon drippings |
| Granulated sugar | 1 cup cream |
| Flour | Chopped parsley |

Slice the tomatoes in ¾-inch slices. Discard top and bottom slices. Sprinkle both sides with salt and pepper and a very little granulated sugar, then dip each slice, both sides, in flour. Fry the tomatoes on both sides, one by one, in a large heavy frying pan in hot butter and bacon drippings. Fry quickly on one side, turn over carefully with pancake turner and place on hot oven-proof platter in the oven while you fry the rest, adding more butter and bacon drippings if necessary. When all are done, pour the cream into the frying pan and stir well, season to taste with salt and coarsely ground black pepper, pour over the tomatoes, sprinkle with chopped parsley, and serve at once. Serves 6 to 8.

### ZUCCHINI WITH WALNUTS

| | |
|---|---|
| 1½ pounds zucchini, unpeeled | 2 tablespoons lemon juice |
| ½ cup sliced scallions | ½ teaspoon salt |
| ½ cup salad oil | ½ cup water |
| ¼ cup dry white wine | ½ cup coarsely chopped walnuts |

Cut zucchini in ½-inch slices. Sauté zucchini and scallions in oil for 5 minutes. Add wine, lemon juice, salt and water. Simmer for 5 minutes. Add walnuts. Serves 6.

*Ripe olives taste better if you soak them overnight in olive oil with a small clove of garlic.*

110

## BAKED ZUCCHINI AND TOMATOES

| | |
|---|---|
| 8 to 10 large juicy tomatoes | 2 small bay leaves |
| 1 very large zucchini, or 6 to 8 | 1 can beef consomme |
| small ones | 2 or 3 tablespoons butter |
| 3 onions, sliced fine | 1 small clove garlic (optional) |
| Salt and pepper | 4 tablespoons olive oil |
| ½ teaspoon dried sweet basil, | Chopped parsley |
| crumbled fine | |

Butter a large oval baking dish. Scald the tomatoes and remove their skins. Place them side by side in the dish. Slice zucchini in one-inch thick pieces. Remove seeds and parboil in salted water 10 to 15 minutes. If you have used the large zucchini, cut the slices in half and cut off the skin. The young small ones may be used unpeeled. Cover the tomatoes with the onion slices, and sprinkle with salt and pepper. Now add the zucchini, arranging them prettily. Again sprinkle lightly with salt and pepper, and add the sweet basil and bay leaves. Pour the can of beef consomme over all and dot with butter. If you like garlic, either bury a small clove of it in the dish, or squeeze the garlic through a garlic press and add to the dish. Trickle the olive oil over the surface. Place in 450° oven and bake for about 2 hours, basting frequently with its own juice. Sprinkle with chopped parsley and serve. Serves 6 to 8.

### FLAMING YAMS

| | |
|---|---|
| Grated rind of 2 oranges | 1 teaspoon cinnamon |
| ¾ cup dark brown sugar | ½ teaspoon cloves |
| ¼ cup dark rum | ¼ teaspoon ginger |
| 6 cooked yams, sliced | 2 tablespoons butter |

Grease a 1½-quart casserole well with butter. Sprinkle with half the orange rind, ¼ cup brown sugar and 2 tablespoons rum. Layer half the sliced yams; sprinkle with ¼ cup brown sugar, ½ teaspoon cinnamon, ¼ teaspoon clove, ⅛ teaspoon ginger. Add another layer of yams and sprinkle with remaining brown sugar, orange rind, cinnamon, cloves and ginger. Dot with butter; bake in 350° oven 45 minutes or until brown. Heat remaining 2 tablespoons rum; pour over hot casserole, and set aflame. Serves 6.

*To color cocoanut, fill a glass jar half full, sprinkle in a few drops of coloring, cover jar and shake.*

111

# Bread

# The Words about Bread

Of all the words in the culinary spectrum the most powerful has to be bread. And yet there is a paradox: "Man cannot live by bread alone." Way back there in 1951 when I wrote my first cookbook and my thoughts on the philosophy of food and living were just beginning to take form, I wrote a piece about bread. On re-examining the bit, I find I still like it and it still expresses my personal feelings about bread. For bread is an intimate and personal food for all of us and closely associated with things near and dear to us. One of my fondest memories comes from my childhood association with bread. If you haven't experienced it, you haven't lived. I can remember coming home from school through the winter's blustery, wind-driven snow to the warmth of our North Dakota kitchen. Even as a boy I wore glasses. I remember when I would first open the door and the warm air from the wood-burning stove would hit the lens and my glasses would steam over and my world would be lost temporarily. But suddenly from out of the depths of that great iron monster would come an aroma—an aroma which to this day defies description and, even as I write this, seems to come from the innards of my typewriter. The wonderful, salty, buttery, pungent, yeasty aroma of freshly baking bread. And when the bread was done, my mother would pile the steaming loaves on the kitchen table and cover them oh-so-gently with a clean dish towel. And if I had been a good boy, she would let me slice a thick heel from one of the loaves. I would douse it with the sweet, fresh butter our farmer friend used to bring every week. And I would pile it high with mother's home-

115

made chokecherry jam. I don't ever expect to taste anything like that again. These days we use mixes and we make "quick" breads; or we do tricks with already baked bread. The demand for bread recipes is so little I don't even include one in this book. It seems strange we do not bake more bread these days. I used to hate that old wood-burning stove with a passion because I had to carry every piece of kindling; I had to chop and tote every stick of wood. Even my mother has been known, but only on very rare occasion, to whisper a "damn" because the oven didn't give even heat and the loaves sometimes came out higher on one end. Now we have the wonderful modern ovens. There is no wood to chop and carry. And with all these conveniences, we do not bake bread.

Shame on us!

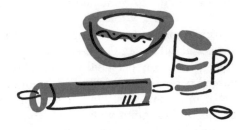

Three party tricks with bread.

### HERB BREAD

| 1 loaf unsliced white bread | Brown wrapping paper |

*Herb Butter:*
¼ pound soft butter
2 tablespoons chopped parsley
2 tablespoons chopped chives
  or green onion tops

1 tablespoon chopped celery
  leaves
1 teaspoon herbs (use sweet
  basil, oregano or thyme)
½ teaspoon lemon juice

Blend herb butter ingredients well. Trim off the ends, side and top crusts of the bread loaf, leaving the bottom crust. Slice bread in 1-inch slices down to the bottom crust. Spread the slices thickly with the herb butter. Wrap in a double thickness of the plain brown wrapping paper and tie with string. If possible, let the wrapped loaf stand overnight in the refrigerator. Bake in a 350° oven for 30 minutes. Unwrap and serve.

### TOMATO ONION CHEESE BREAD

1 long loaf sour dough
  French bread
Soft butter or margarine
Tomato slices

Thin onion slices
Processed American cheese
  slices

Slice ½-inch thick slices down to the bottom of the loaf of bread, leaving the loaf held together by the bottom crust. Spread with butter or margarine. Insert tomato, onion and cheese slices between each bread slice. Wrap in aluminum foil. Bake in 350° oven 30 minutes or until bread is hot and cheese melted.

### GARLIC CHEESE TOAST

1 loaf sour dough French bread
Butter or margarine
Mashed garlic

Parmesan cheese
Paprika

---

*To keep those unsightly and hard-to-remove lumps from forming in creamed gravy and soups use a little salt in the flour when thickening.*

Blend butter or margarine with mashed garlic and let stand for a half hour. Slice bread lengthwise and then cut individual slices down to the bottom of the loaf, but not through. Spread with garlic butter and sprinkle with cheese and paprika. Place a half loaf, butter side down, on foil. Place the other half loaf, butter side up, on top. Wrap in foil. Place loaf under a high broiler, three inches from heat, for 10 minutes on each side. Remove foil and serve.

### SOURDOUGH STARTER

1 cup milk                    1 cup flour

Place the milk in glass jar or crock and allow to stand at room temperature for 24 hours. (Do not use metal container). Stir in flour. Leave uncovered in a warm place for two to five days, until it has bubbles and is sour. About 80°, like near a gas pilot light is best. If it starts to dry out use enough tepid water to bring it back to its original consistency. Once it has a sour aroma and is full of bubbles, it is ready to use.

Each time you use part of your starter, replenish it with a mixture of equal amounts of milk and flour. Try to maintain 1½ cups of starter. Leave at room temperature for several hours or overnight until it is full of bubbles, then cover and store in the refrigerator.

The starter is best if used once a week. If it is not used but about once every 2 or 3 weeks, spoon out and discard about half of the starter and replenish it as described. If you do not plan to use the starter for several weeks, it is best to freeze it, allowing 24 hours for thawing.

### SOURDOUGH BREAD

2 cups starter                    1 tablespoon sugar
2½ to 3 cups flour                ¼ cup melted butter or lard
1 teaspoon salt

Put starter into bowl. Add enough of the flour to make a soft dough, along with the salt, sugar and butter. Knead dough well until it squeaks.

---

*To substitute for sour milk or buttermilk, add a couple of teaspoons of vinegar to a cup of sweet milk.*

Allow to rise in a warm spot. (If starter is very sour to your taste, add ½ teaspoon soda dissolved in 1 tablespoon warm water at this point and work it into the dough). Form 1 loaf, use the rest for biscuits. Allow to rise until double. Bake in 370° oven for 45 minutes until done.

Be sure to save enough starter from each batch to hold over and start the next baking.

## OLD COUNTRY SODA BREAD

2 tablespoons honey
4 ounces butter
½ cup buttermilk
5 cups flour (3 cups white flour, 2 cups wheat or brown flour)

1 teaspoon salt
1 teaspoon baking soda
2 heaping teaspoons baking powder
2 eggs, beaten

In a sauce pan melt butter and honey together over medium heat. When hot, combine with buttermilk. Mix all dry ingredients together. Add to liquid mixture along with eggs and knead. Cut dough in quarters and place on floured cookie or pizza pan. Bake in 325° oven for 55 minutes.

## BISHOP'S BREAD

2¾ cups sifted all-purpose flour
3 teaspoons baking powder
1 teaspoon salt
½ cup soft butter or margarine

1 cup light brown sugar, firmly packed
2 eggs
1 cup milk

Topping:

½ cup granulated sugar
½ cup sifted all-purpose flour

¼ cup butter or margarine
1 tablespoon cinnamon

Preheat oven to 375°. Then lightly grease a 13x9x2-inch baking pan. Sift flour with baking powder and salt. In large bowl of electric mixer, at medium speed, beat butter with the brown sugar and eggs, beating

*Eliminate waste when measuring molasses by buttering the measuring cup lightly.*

119

until the mixture is very light and fluffy. At low speed, blend in milk, then the flour mixture, beating just to combine. Turn batter into the prepared pan, spreading evenly. Make topping by combining, in small bowl, the granulated sugar, ½ cup flour, ¼ cup butter and cinnamon, and mix till crumbly. Sprinkle over batter. Bake 25 minutes, until a cake tester inserted in the center comes out clean. Let cool slightly in pan on wire rack. Serve bread warm. Serves 16.

### BROWN BREAD

2 cups graham flour
1 cup white flour
1 teaspoon salt
1 teaspoon soda
1 teaspoon baking powder
½ cup brown sugar (packed)
1 cup white sugar

1 cup raisins
1 cup walnuts, chopped
½ cup dark molasses
1½ cups sour milk
2 tablespoons melted
  shortening

Mix all ingredients together, combining the dry ingredients with the moist ones. Bake slowly in greased loaf pan in 350° oven for about 1 hour. This bread is much better served the day after baking.

### BRAN MUFFINS

2 cups all-purpose or whole-
  grain flour
1½ cups bran
2 tablespoons sugar
¼ teaspoon salt
1¼ teaspoons soda
1 to 2 tablespoons grated
  orange rind (optional)

2 cups buttermilk
1 beaten egg
½ cup molasses
2 to 4 tablespoons melted
  butter
1 cup nut meats

Combine flour, bran, sugar, salt, soda and orange rind and stir well. Beat together buttermilk, egg, molasses and melted butter. Combine the dry and the liquid ingredients with a few swift strokes. Fold in the nut meats before the dry ingredients are entirely moist. (½ cup mashed

---

*A little salt sprinkled on whipping cream will help it whip more easily and rapidly. Same thing for egg whites.*

bananas may be added at this time, if desired). Bake at 350° for about 25 minutes. Makes about twenty-two 2-inch muffins.

### ORANGE-PECAN BREAD

2 cups chopped pecans
2 tablespoons grated orange peel
2 oranges
2¾ cups sifted all-purpose flour
2½ teaspoons baking powder

½ teaspoon baking soda
1 teaspoon salt
2 tablespoons butter, margarine or shortening
1 cup honey
1 egg

Chop pecans coarsely. Grate orange peel, enough to make 2 tablespoons. Reserve. Squeeze juice from oranges to make ¾ cup. Sift flour, baking powder, baking soda and salt into a bowl. Mix softened butter with honey until you have a creamy mixture. Now stir unbeaten egg and orange peel into honey mixture. Mix well. Stir sifted dry ingredients alternately with orange juice and honey-butter mixture. Mix thoroughly after each addition. Stir in nuts last of all and spoon into loaf pan, either greased and floured 9x5x3 pan or three little 3½x5 ¾x2¼ pans. Bake at 350° for 45 to 50 minutes.

### ENGLISH WALNUT LOAF

4 cups plain flour
1½ pounds white raisins
1 pound crystallized cherries
½ nutmeg grated
1 heaping teaspoon baking powder
½ pound butter

2 cups sugar
6 egg yolks and whites beaten separately
1 teaspoon vanilla
1 teaspoon cinnamon
4 cups English walnuts (shelled)

Cut raisins or put through coarse food chopper. Mix the raisins and cherries with ⅓ of the flour. Add grated nutmeg and baking powder to rest of the flour. Cream butter and sugar till fluffy. Add well beaten egg yolks. Mix well. Add vanilla and cinnamon. Add flour slowly. Fold in stiffly beaten egg whites. Add nuts, raisins and cherries. Mix well. Bake in large pan 275° for 2½ to 3 hours.

*Soak pecans in salt water for several hours before cracking them. The nutmeats are then easy to remove whole.*

## EGG LADY'S CARROT BREAD

This is the only carrot loaf I ever liked. It comes from Mrs. Roselyn Ponedah, the wife of Bob, who brings us fresh eggs every week.

2 eggs, beaten
¾ cup cooking oil
1 cup sugar
1½ cups grated carrots
   (very, very fine)

1½ cups all-purpose flour
1 teaspoon soda
1 teaspoon cinnamon
1 teaspoon salt
½ cup chopped nuts

Mix all ingredients. Place in greased pan. Bake in 350° oven for 1½ hours.

## BANANA TEA BREAD

1¾ cups sifted flour
2 teaspoons baking powder
¼ teaspoon baking soda
½ teaspoon salt
⅓ cup shortening

⅔ cup sugar
2 eggs, well-beaten
1 cup mashed ripe bananas
   (2 to 3 bananas)

Sift together flour, baking powder, soda and salt. Beat shortening until creamy in mixing bowl. Add sugar gradually and continue beating until light and fluffy. Add eggs and beat well. Add flour mixture alternately with bananas, a small amount at a time, beating after each addition until smooth. Turn into a well-greased bread pan (8½ x 4½ x 3 inches) and bake in a 350° oven about 1 hour, 10 minutes or until bread is done. Makes 1 loaf.

## QUICK CRANBERRY BREAD

1½ cups all-purpose flour
½ teaspoon salt
1 teaspoon soda
1½ cups whole grain flour
¼ cups shortening
½ cup sugar
1 egg

¾ cup unsweetened, cooked,
   mashed cranberry pulp
¼ cup cranberry juice
1 cup buttermilk
1 cup broken nut meats
Grated rind of 1 orange

---

*Disagreeable odors can be eliminated when cooking cabbage and greens by adding salt to the water and leaving the pan uncovered.*

Preheat oven to 350°. Sift before measuring the all-purpose flour. Resift with salt and soda. Add whole grain flour. Cream shortening with sugar. Beat in the egg. Add mashed cranberry pulp and cranberry juice. Add the sifted ingredients alternately to the butter mixture with buttermilk. Stir the batter with a few swift strokes, until just blended. Fold in nut meats and grated rind. Place the dough in a greased loaf pan. Bake the bread for about 1¼ hours. Let it cool in the pan.

### BLUEBERRY CRUMB MUFFINS

¼ cup shortening  
¼ cup sugar  
1 egg, well beaten  
1 cup flour  
3 teaspoons baking powder

½ teaspoon salt  
1 cup fine dry bread crumbs  
1 cup milk  
1 cup fresh blueberries

Cream together the shortening and sugar until light. Stir in the well beaten egg. Sift flour, measure, and sift with the baking powder and salt. Mix bread crumbs with the flour mixture, then add it alternately with the milk to the creamed mixture. Lightly stir in the blueberries. Spoon into 12 well-greased muffin pans, filling them about two thirds full. Bake in a 375° oven for about 25 minutes. Makes 12 medium-sized muffins.

### DATE PECAN MUFFINS

2 eggs, well beaten  
1 cup raw sugar or brown sugar  
½ teaspoon vanilla  
⅔ cup flour  
¼ teaspoon each baking powder

and salt  
¾ cup finely chopped dates  
¾ cup finely chopped pecans or other nut meats

Combine eggs with sugar and vanilla. Sift the flour, measure; add baking powder and salt and sift into egg mixture with the dates and nuts. Mix until well blended and spoon into buttered small muffin pans, filling them about ⅔ full. Bake in a 400° oven for about 10 minutes or until lightly browned. Remove from pans and cool. Makes 16.

*Cake icings will not sugar if a pinch of salt is added while icing is being cooked.*

123

## MAPLE-WALNUT MUFFINS

2 cups packaged biscuit mix  
2 tablespoons sugar  
¼ cup chopped walnuts  
1 egg  

¼ cup milk  
½ cup maple-flavored syrup  
2 tablespoons salad oil  
1 teaspoon maple flavoring  

In large bowl, combine biscuit mix with sugar and walnuts, mixing well. Beat egg slightly in small bowl. Add milk, syrup, oil and maple flavoring; mix well. Make a well in center of dry ingredients. Pour in milk mixture all at once, mixing with fork just until dry ingredients are moistened—batter will be lumpy. Pour into greased muffin pan cups, filling about ⅔ full. Bake in 400° oven for 15 minutes, or until cake tester inserted in center comes out clean. Serve warm. Makes 12 muffins.

## CHEESE-CORN MEAL BISCUITS

¾ cup milk  
½ cup yellow corn meal  
1 cup flour  
1 tablespoon baking powder  

¾ teaspoon salt  
3 tablespoons butter  
¾ cup grated Cheddar cheese  
1 egg yolk, slightly beaten  

Scald the milk and add corn meal. Mix well and cool. Sift together twice the flour, baking powder and salt. Cut the butter into the flour mixture until it resembles fine bread crumbs. Add cheese to milk-corn meal mixture. Mix thoroughly. Turn out onto a lightly floured board. Knead 2-3 minutes. Roll out ½ inch thick. Cut with a 1¼" cookie cutter. Place on lightly greased baking sheets. Brush tops with egg yolk. Bake in 425° oven for about 15 minutes or until golden. Remove and cool on wire cake racks. Serve warm, split and buttered. Makes about 36 biscuits.

*To remove lime deposits in glass cookware or a teakettle, boil in a light vinegar solution for ten minutes.*

# Sugar and Spice

# The Words about Sugar and Spice

These are the nice words. The mere use brings a look of anticipation and a smile. From birth man's stomach seems to want to eat at least three times a day, to renew the strength he spends in labor or, as happens sometimes, in idleness. Alexandre Dumas, who was one of the world's great gourmets, tells us that eating has been the great preoccupation of both primitive and civilized man. But the savage eats from need while the civilized man eats from desire. This book is written for civilized man. The savage has no need to whet his appetite. I think you'll agree with Dumas that there are three types of appetite. 1. The appetite that comes from hunger. It makes no fuss over the food that satisfies it. If it is great enough, a piece of raw meat will appease it as easily as a roasted pheasant. 2. Appetite aroused by a succulent dish prepared so beautifully that it can stimulate hunger. 3. The appetite that is extra-aroused after normal hunger has been satisfied. If ever a dish will do that job, it is a rich, calorie-laden dessert. I've chosen to embellish the desserts section with some confections, nuts, punches and liquors for the simple reason that I wanted to include them and there was no place else to put them. Some of them like the green tomato pie have just about disappeared from cookbooks. Alison's gingerbread is here along with the Brown Derby's famous grapefruit cake. The cookies are in answer to requests from listeners to our KNX radio show. The punch bowl recipes answer requests from my friends who drink. And "Kahlua Under the Sink" and "Cherry Booze on A High, Safe Shelf" are just plain fun.

127

### EGGNOG PIE

1 9" baked pie shell, or crumb
crust shell
2 tablespoons (2 envelopes)
unflavored gelatin
½ cup milk
2 cups prepared eggnog mix
½ teaspoon grated nutmeg

½ teaspoon cinnamon
2 tablespoons brandy
2 tablespoons rum
1 teaspoon vanilla
1 cup whipping cream, whipped
1 cup diced mixed candied
fruitcake fruits

Soften gelatin in milk and melt over hot water in a double boiler until gelatin is dissolved. Let cool and add to eggnog mix, along with spices, brandy, rum and vanilla. Fold in whipped cream and fruits. Pour the whole mixture into the baked pie shell and refrigerate 3 hours to allow pie to set. Garnish with nuts or pieces of fruit.

### GRAPE PIE

1 quart ripe grapes (blue, or
flavorsome grapes,
preferred), stemmed
½ to 1 cup sugar, depending
on the acid, or sweetness of
your grapes (part honey may

be used instead of sugar)
1½ tablespoons lemon juice
1 tablespoon grated rind
2 tablespoons instant tapioca
Uncooked pastry

(if using green grapes, cook whole, using grapes when about size of green peas and use perhaps a bit more lemon).

Slip grapes from skins (after boiling skins slip off easily), save skins, cook pulp till seeds are loose, then put pulp through coarse sieve removing seeds. Mix skins, pulp and other ingredients, let stand few minutes. Pour this into lined pie pans, cover top with strips of pastry, lattice effect. Lay long narrow strip around edge of pan, crimping it into the bottom crust with a fork. Bake 350° oven 45 to 50 minutes. Good hot, with honey and butter, or chilled with whipped cream.

---

*When using an aluminum double boiler, a half teaspoon of cream of tartar or vinegar in the lower compartment will prevent discoloration.*

## PUMPKIN CHIFFON PIE

| | |
|---|---|
| 1 envelope unflavored gelatin | 2 egg yolks |
| ½ cup milk | 2 egg whites |
| ¾ cup brown sugar, firmly packed | 1½ teaspoons vanilla |
| | ⅓ cup sugar |
| ½ teaspoon salt | ½ teaspoon grated orange rind |
| 1 teaspoon cinnamon | ½ teaspoon grated lemon rind |
| ½ teaspoon ginger | ½ cup whipping cream, whipped |
| 1 can (about 1 lb.) pumpkin (1½ cups) | 1 cup coarsely chopped pecan meats |

9-inch baked pastry shell or crumb crust.

Soften gelatin in ¼ cup milk, then combine gelatin mixture with brown sugar, salt, cinnamon, ginger, pumpkin, egg yolks and remaining ¼ cup milk in saucepan. Cook over medium heat, stirring constantly until mixture comes to boiling. Do not boil. Cool; chill until mixture is thoroughly cold and will mound when spooned. Beat egg whites until soft peaks form; add vanilla; add sugar slowly, continue beating until mixture is stiff and glossy. Fold into pumpkin mixture; fold in orange rind, lemon rind, whipping cream and pecan meats. Pile into crust; chill several hours, or until set. Garnish with orange sections, additional whipped cream and pecans, if desired.

## PUMPKIN PECAN PIE

(2 9-inch pies)

*Dough:*

| | |
|---|---|
| 3 cups flour | 1 egg, slightly beaten |
| 1 teaspoon salt | Cold water |
| 1 cup shortening | 2 tablespoons butter |
| 3 tablespoons unstrained lemon juice | 6 tablespoons chopped pecans |

Mix and sift together flour and salt. Blend in shortening. Add lemon juice to egg and add to flour mixture with enough cold water to hold the dough together. Chill for 15 minutes and roll out thinly. Line two 9-inch pie plates.

---

*Rub your pancake griddle with a little bag of salt instead of grease. The pancakes will not stick, and the salt will prevent smoke and odor.*

Spread each with 1 tablespoon butter, and sprinkle with 3 tablespoons chopped pecans. Fill the pie shells to ¼ inch from the top with the filling.

*Filling:*

| | |
|---|---|
| 6 eggs | Milk (to moisten spices) |
| ½ cup molasses | 2 cups hot milk |
| 1½ cups brown sugar | 3 cups mashed pumpkin pulp |
| 1 scant teaspoon each; salt, | 6 tablespoons chopped pecans |
| grated nutmeg, ground | 2 tablespoons butter |
| ginger, ground cinnamon | |

Beat eggs, molasses and brown sugar with a rotary beater for at least 5 minutes. Moisten salt, nutmeg, ginger and cinnamon with a little milk and stir until smooth. Stir the hot milk into the spices. Mix thoroughly and add the spiced milk to the egg mixture. Add the pumpkin a little at a time, mixing well after each addition. Fill the prepared pie shells and bake in a moderate oven for about 15 minutes. Then sprinkle over each pie 3 tablespoons chopped pecans and 1 tablespoon melted butter. Bake for 35 to 45 minutes, or until the filling is set and browned.

### CRANBERRY CHIFFON PIE

| | |
|---|---|
| 2 envelopes unflavored gelatin | Red food coloring, optional |
| ½ cup cold water | 3 egg whites |
| 1½ cups cranberries | 1 baked 9-inch pie shell |
| ¼ cup water | ½ cup heavy cream |
| 1 cup sugar | 2 teaspoons sugar |
| ½ teaspoon salt | ½ teaspoon vanilla |
| ¼ cup orange juice | |
| 2 teaspoons grated orange peel | |

Soften gelatin in ½ cup cold water. Wash cranberries and combine with ¼ cup water in saucepan. Cover and cook just until skins pop, about 10 minutes. Add ½ cup sugar, salt and softened gelatin. Mix well. Stir in orange juice and peel. Add food coloring to tint deeper pink, if wished. Chill until mixture begins to thicken. Beat egg whites

*To dust food with flour, use a large salt shaker and sprinkle lightly instead of dipping the food into the flour. It's a lot less mess.*

until soft peaks form. Gradually beat in the remaining ½ cup sugar. Fold into cranberry mixture. Spoon into baked pie shell. Chill until ready to serve. Whip cream with sugar and vanilla and serve on pie.

## GREEN TOMATO PIE

| | |
|---|---|
| Pastry for two crusts | ¾ tablespoon cinnamon |
| Green tomatoes (2 cups) | 1 tablespoon vinegar |
| ½ cup raisins | 1 tablespoon grated lemon rind |
| ½ teaspoon cloves | ⅛ teaspoon grated nutmeg |
| ½ cup brown sugar | 2 tablespoons butter |
| 1 tablespoon salt | 2 tablespoons brown sugar |

Skin and chop tomatoes and add remaining ingredients, stir well. Line pie-tin with pastry, pour in mixture, cover with top crust, dot with butter and sprinkle lightly with brown sugar. Bake 45 to 50 minutes at 375°.

## LIME CHIFFON PIE IN MERINGUE

| | |
|---|---|
| Baked meringue shell | Green food coloring |
| 4 eggs, separated | (optional) |
| ¼ teaspoon cream of tartar | 1 tablespoon grated lime peel |
| 1½ cups sugar | 2 cups heavy cream |
| ¼ teaspoon salt | 2 tablespoons Triple Sec |
| ⅓ cup lime juice | |

Bring egg whites to room temperature, add cream of tartar and beat until frothy. Gradually add 1 cup sugar, continuing to beat until very stiff and glossy. Spread in a lightly greased 9-inch pie pan, making depression in center with back of spoon for shell shape. Bake at 275°, 20 minutes, then increase heat to 300° and bake 40 minutes. Cool slowly. Beat egg yolks well in top of double boiler, then beat in salt, ½ cup sugar and lime juice. Cook over hot, not boiling, water 10 minutes or until thickened. Cool. Tint pale green with food coloring, if desired. Fold in lime peel, Triple Sec and 1 cup of the cream, which has been whipped. Spread into baked meringue shell. Whip remaining 1 cup of cream, sweeten, if desired, and spread over filling. Chill at least 4 hours before serving.

*Use a pan the same size or larger than the burner or the heating element. Pans that are too small are heat wasters.*

## TWO-CRUST LEMON PIE

Pastry for double crust pie
1¼ cups sugar
2 tablespoons flour
Dash salt
¼ cup soft butter or margarine
3 eggs

1 teaspoon grated lemon peel
1 medium lemon, very thinly
sliced
½ cup water
2 teaspoons sugar
½ teaspoon cinnamon

Line 8-inch pie plate with half the pastry. Combine sugar, flour and salt. Blend in soft butter and mix well. Reserve about 1 teaspoon egg white and beat remaining eggs well. Add to first mixture. Add lemon peel and slices and water to sugar mixture. Blend well and turn into pastry-lined plate. Cover pie with pastry, cut slits in pastry, seal and flute edges. Brush top of pie with reserved egg white. Mix sugar and cinnamon and sprinkle over pie. Bake at 400° 30 to 35 minutes.

## BROWN DERBY GRAPEFRUIT CAKE

1½ cups sifted cake flour
¾ cup sugar
1½ teaspoons baking powder
½ teaspoon salt
¼ cup water

¼ cup vegetable oil
3 eggs, separated
3 tablespoons grapefruit juice
½ teaspoon grated lemon rind
¼ teaspoon cream of tartar

Sift together flour, sugar, baking powder and salt into mixing bowl. Make a well in center of dry ingredients. Add water, oil, egg yolks, grapefruit juice and lemon rind. Beat until very smooth. Beat egg whites and cream of tartar separately until whites are stiff but not dry. Gradually pour egg yolk mixture over whites, folding gently with a rubber spatula until just blended. Do not stir mixture. Pour into an ungreased 9 inch round cake pan. Bake in a 350° oven, 25 to 30 minutes, or until cake springs back when lightly touched with finger. Invert pan on cake rack until cool. Run spatula around edge of cake. Carefully remove from pan. With a serrated knife, gently cut layer in half. Frost with Grapefruit Cream Cheese Frosting.

---

*Always prepare all foods at room temperature. This is most important in meat cookery.*

132

## CREAM CHEESE FROSTING

2 3-ounce packages cream cheese
2 teaspoons lemon juice
1 teaspoon grated lemon rind
¾ cup powdered sugar, sifted

6 to 8 drops yellow food coloring
1 (1-pound) can grapefruit sections, well drained

Let cream cheese soften at room temperature. Beat cheese until fluffy. Add lemon juice and rind. Gradually blend in sugar. Beat until well blended. Crush broken grapefruit sections to measure 2 teaspoons. Blend into frosting. Spread frosting on bottom half of cake. Top with several grapefruit sections. Cover with second layer. Frost top and sides, garnish with remaining grapefruit sections.

## HOLIDAY SPECIAL FRUIT CAKE

½ cup sifted all-purpose flour
½ teaspoon salt
½ teaspoon baking powder
⅛ teaspoon allspice
⅛ teaspoon nutmeg
⅓ cup shortening
3 tablespoon sugar
2 eggs, unbeaten
3 tablespoons honey
2 tablespoons orange juice or Curaçao, Triple Sec or

Cointreau
1 cup diced preserved pineapple
½ cup diced preserved orange peel
½ cup diced preserved lemon peel
¼ cup diced preserved citron
1 cup candied cherries
3½ cups pecan halves

Preheat oven to 300°. Line a 1¼-inch deep by 8-inch layer cake pan with two thicknesses of waxed paper; then grease. Sift together the first five ingredients. Cream shortening and sugar, then add eggs and honey and beat until very light and fluffy—about 4 minutes. Then blend in alternately the flour mixture with the orange juice—just until smooth. Spread ⅓ of the batter in the cake pan. Add the fruits and nuts to the rest of the batter, saving a few cherries and nuts for decorating the top of the cake. Pile fruit-batter mixture on top of batter in pan and pack down. Decorate with cherries and nuts. Cover

*You'll use much less sugar in iced tea or coffee if you dissolve the sugar in hot water ahead of time.*

with brown paper and tie securely. Set in shallow pan of hot water. Water should be only ¼ of the depth of the cake pan. Bake one hour. Remove from water. Bake one more hour. When done, remove paper from top and brush with hot corn syrup. Cool on wire rack and tear off wax paper.

### HEIRLOOM FRUITCAKE
(From the Los Angeles Times)

2 pounds candied cherries
2 pounds candied pineapple
½ pound citron
½ pound candied orange peel
½ pound candied lemon peel
11-ounces shelled pecans
2 pounds pitted dates
2 pounds golden raisins
1 pound dark raisins
1 pound currants
1 pint brandy
1 pint rum
1 pound butter or margarine
1 pound brown sugar

1 dozen large eggs
3 teaspoons vanilla
Juice of 1 large lemon
Juice of 1 large orange
4 cups sifted flour
2 teaspoons baking powder
1 teaspoon soda
1 teaspoon nutmeg
1 teaspoon allspice
3 teaspoons cinnamon
1 12-ounce jar apple or grape jelly
1 cup brandy, wine or grape juice

Dice candied fruits and peels, break nuts into coarse pieces and snip dates and raisins in small pieces with scissors dipped in hot water. Soak all fruits overnight in brandy and rum. Combine fruits and nuts in large bowl and toss together with enough additional flour to coat well. Cream together butter and brown sugar until fluffy. Add eggs, one at a time, beating well after each addition. Stir in vanilla, lemon and orange juices. Sift together flour, baking powder, soda, nutmeg, allspice and cinnamon. Beat together jelly and brandy until smooth. Alternately add flour mixture and jelly mixture to the creamed mixture, blending well. Stir in fruit and nut mixture. Dough will be very stiff, so a wooden paddle or scraper will mix most efficiently. Grease pans, line with brown paper and grease the paper. Turn batter into pans, filling three-fourths full and smoothing tops. Bake at 200° until

---

*Add finely grated raw carrot to vegetable soup before serving; it gives a rich color and adds flavor and texture.*

134

a wood pick inserted near centers of cakes comes out clean. Loaf cakes will take about 2½ hours, or 10-inch tube pans about 6½ hours. Cool cakes in pans. Remove cakes from pans and pour a little wine over tops. Wrap in cloth soaked in wine, then wrap in foil. Or, glaze tops and let thoroughly dry. Wrap in cloth soaked in wine, then wrap in foil. Store in a cool place, but not the refrigerator, at least a month before serving. Makes about 10 pounds.

### FRUITCAKE GLAZE

1 cup sugar                    ½ cup water
⅓ cup light corn syrup

Combine sugar, corn syrup and water in saucepan. Cook, stirring constantly, until syrup spins a fine thread (200° on candy thermometer). Brush hot syrup over cooled fruitcakes. Let dry until tacky, then arrange candied cherries, citron or pineapple in design on top of cake and brush with more glaze. Let glaze dry thoroughly before covering cake for storage.

### ALISON'S GINGERBREAD

Into ½ cup boiling water put:
½ cup shortening.

Set aside.

Sift:
1½ cups flour                  ½ teaspoon ground cloves
1 teaspoon soda                ½ teaspoon ground ginger
1 teaspoon salt                ½ teaspoon ground allspice
½ teaspoon cinnamon

Put into bowl at one time:
1 egg                          Sifted dry ingredients
½ cup white sugar              Shortening and water
½ cup molasses                 1 cup raisins

Mix well. Pour into greased and floured pan. Bake at 350° for 20 minutes.

*Sugar your donuts and cookies evenly by placing them in a paper bag with a little powdered sugar and then shaking.*

### BROWN BETTY

1 cup dry bread or graham
  cracker crumbs
¼ cup melted butter
¾ cup packed brown sugar
1 teaspoon cinnamon
¼ teaspoon each nutmeg and
  cloves
½ teaspoon salt

1 teaspoon grated lemon rind
1 teaspoon vanilla
3 tablespoons lemon juice
2½ cups diced or sliced apples,
  or peaches, cherries or
  cranberries
4 tablespoons water
½ cup raisins

Combine crumbs and melted butter. Line the bottom of a 9 inch by 9 inch baking dish with ⅓ of the crumb mixture. Sift brown sugar, cinnamon, nutmeg, cloves and salt. Add lemon rind and vanilla. Place ½ of the apples in the dish. Cover the layer with ½ of the sugar mixture. Sprinkle with 1 tablespoon lemon juice. Add 2 tablespoons water. Cover the apples with ⅓ of the crumb mixture and ¼ cup of the raisins. Add the remaining apples and sprinkle them as before with the remaining sugar mixture, and 2 tablespoons lemon juice, 2 tablespoons water and the remaining ¼ cup raisins. Place the last ⅓ of the crumb mixture on top. Cover the dish and bake for about 40 minutes in a 350° oven until the apples are nearly tender. Remove cover, increase heat to 400° and permit pudding to brown for about 15 minutes. Serve hot.

### ORANGE TORTE

1 angel food cake
½ cup frozen orange juice
  concentrate, defrosted
1 quart vanilla ice cream
1 large banana, diced

¼ cup whipping cream,
  whipped
1 cup toasted cocoanut
Orange segments

Line a 1½ or 2 quart bowl with plastic wrap. Break cake in chunks about the size of a walnut and layer in bottom of bowl. Soften ice cream to spreading consistency and spread a layer over the cake. Sprinkle with a tablespoon of the orange concentrate. Intersperse banana. Repeat layers until all is used, ending with cake. Cover bowl

*Remove the cookies from a baking sheet with a spatula as soon as they're done. Don't pile them or they'll stick together.*

with wrap or foil and freeze in freezer. To serve, remove wrap and place upside down on serving plate, frozen. Remove wrap. Cover with mounds of whipped cream; sprinkle with toasted cocoanut and garnish with orange segments. (To toast cocoanut, place in shallow pan in 350° oven; stir or shake frequently until cocoanut is brown. Be careful it doesn't burn.)

## BIG DESSERT

1 #2 can crushed pineapple
1 4-ounce box marshmallows, finely cut
1 8-ounce bottle maraschino cherries
1 envelope plain gelatin

1 cup milk
1 cup chopped blanched almonds
1 pint heavy cream, whipped
1 10-inch (large) angel food cake

Combine pineapple, marshmallows and cherries including juices (save a few cherries for decoration). Let stand 6 hours or overnight. Soften gelatin in ½ cup cold milk 5 minutes; add ½ cup hot milk. Chill until slightly thickened. Add fruit mixture and almonds; fold in whipped cream. Cut angel food cake into two layers. Put layers together with mixture and frost top and sides. If you still have mixture left, drop in middle. Chill cake before serving. Decorate with cherries and almond halves. Serves 20.

## ALMOND FRIED CREAM

2 cups heavy cream
1 tablespoon rum
½ teaspoon salt
4 tablespoons brown sugar
¼ cup ground almonds
¼ cup cornstarch

¼ cup milk
3 egg yolks
⅛ pound butter
2 jiggers rum
Egg and crumbs

In the top of a double boiler scald cream with the rum, salt, brown sugar and ground almonds. Add milk and egg yolks to cornstarch, combine with cream mixture. Cook over hot water until thick and

*If your icebox cookie dough crumbles when you take it from the refrigerator, let it stand at room temperature for a half hour.*

smooth. Pour into shallow pan and chill. Then cut in squares, dip in eggs and crumbs and again chill. When ready to serve, cook in blazer in butter, browning both sides. Just before serving pour on 2 jiggers of rum and set on fire. Serves 6 to 8.

### ALMOND COOKIES

| | |
|---|---|
| 1 cup butter or margarine | 3 cups sifted flour |
| 1 cup sugar | 1½ teaspoons baking soda |
| 1 egg, beaten | ¼ cup light corn syrup |
| 3 tablespoons almond extract | 1 cup blanched almonds |

Cream butter and sugar until light and fluffy. Add beaten egg and almond extract and continue beating. Slowly stir in flour, baking soda and corn syrup; mix until smooth. Form the dough into 1-inch balls and place on a baking sheet. Flatten each ball into a thick cookie with the bottom of a tumbler. Place an almond in the center of each cookie. Bake in a 375° oven for 15 to 20 minutes or until golden brown. Makes about 4 dozen cookies.

### BOURBON BALLS

| | |
|---|---|
| 2 tablespoons cocoa | 2½ cups vanilla wafer crumbs |
| 1 cup powdered sugar | or leftover cake or cookie |
| ¼ cup bourbon (brandy or rum, or ⅛ cup each) | crumbs |
| | 1 cup broken nut meats |
| 2 tablespoons light corn syrup | ½ cup powdered sugar |

Sift together cocoa and 1 cup powdered sugar. Combine and stir in bourbon, corn syrup. Add crumbs and nuts and mix thoroughly. Roll into small balls. Dredge in ½ cup powdered sugar. Store in air tight containers. Flavor improves on standing.

### CHINESE CHEWS

| | |
|---|---|
| 1 cup granulated sugar | 1 cup chopped dates |
| ¾ cup flour | 1 cup chopped walnuts |
| 1 teaspoon baking powder | 2 eggs, beaten lightly |
| ¼ teaspoon salt | Powdered sugar |

*Always pour a little salt in the water when poaching eggs. This will set the white, giving the eggs a better appearance when served.*

Mix dry ingredients together. Add dates, nuts and eggs. Mix well. Spread out thinly on a greased cookie sheet. Bake in 325° oven for 20 minutes. Cut in squares and roll in powdered sugar.

### 5-MINUTE COOKIES

| | |
|---|---|
| 2 cups sugar | ½ cup milk |
| ¼ teaspoon salt | 1 teaspoon vanilla |
| 2½ tablespoons cocoa | 1 cup crunchy peanut butter |
| 1 cube butter | 3 cups quick cooking oatmeal |

Place sugar, salt, cocoa, butter and milk in saucepan and bring to a rolling boil. Remove from heat. Add remaining ingredients and mix well. Drop from teaspoon onto wax paper. Cool.

### MOLASSES CRISPS

| | |
|---|---|
| ½ cup dark molasses | baking powder |
| ¼ cup sugar | ½ teaspoon each fresh ground |
| 6 tablespoons butter | nutmeg and cloves |
| 1 tablespoon milk | 2 teaspoons cinnamon |
| 2 cups all-purpose flour | Pecan or blanched almond |
| ½ teaspoon salt | halves |
| ½ teaspoon double-acting | |

Heat molasses to the boiling point in top of double boiler over hot water. Remove from heat, add sugar, butter, milk, flour, salt, baking powder, nutmeg, cloves and cinnamon and beat until blended. Form into roll, wrap in foil and cool until firm. To form, slice very thin, and if necessary, pat thin on tin with fingers until translucent. Press a pecan or blanched almond halve in the center of each cookie. Preheat oven to 325° and bake for 10 to 12 minutes on greased cookie sheets.

### PEANUT COOKIES

| | |
|---|---|
| 1 cup shortening | 2 eggs |
| 2 cups brown sugar | 1 teaspoon vanilla |

*Grated orange peel added to the molasses gives your gingerbread a little extra pazazz.*

½ teaspoon almond extract     1 teaspoon baking powder
2 cups corn flakes     1 teaspoon soda
1 cup quick cooking oatmeal     1½ cups salted Spanish peanuts
2½ cups flour

Mix shortening, brown sugar, eggs, vanilla and almond extract well with electric beater. Add corn flakes and oatmeal and mix well. Sift flour, baking powder and soda together. Add and mix well. Add peanuts and mix. Drop by teaspoon onto greased cookie sheet. Bake 12 minutes in 350° oven. Makes 9 dozen.

### ROCKS

1 cup butter     1 teaspoon vanilla
1 cup shortening     5 cups flour
2 cups brown sugar     1 level teaspoon soda dissolved
4 eggs     in 1 tablespoon hot water
½ teaspoon salt     1 cup chopped walnuts
3 teaspoons cinnamon     1 cup seeded raisins

Cream butter and shortening and sugar. Add eggs one at a time. Blend in other ingredients in order given. Drop from a spoon onto an ungreased cookie sheet. Bake in 400° oven for about 15 minutes. Yield 10 dozen.

### ROBIN'S SANDIES

1 cup butter     2 cups sifted flour
⅓ cup sugar     1 cup chopped pecans
2 teaspoons water     Powdered sugar
2 teaspoons vanilla

Cream butter and sugar well. Add water, vanilla; mix well; then add flour and pecans. Chill. Shape into balls the size of walnuts. Bake on ungreased cookie sheet in a 325° oven for 20 minutes. Cool slightly and roll in powdered sugar. Makes 5 dozen.

---

*To keep unused cake fresh, cover the cut surface with a strip of waxed paper.*

140

## THREE LAYER NO-BAKE COOKIES

*First Layer*

½ cup butter
¼ cup sugar
¼ cup cocoa
1 teaspoon vanilla
1 egg, slightly beaten

2 cups finely crushed graham
  cracker crumbs
1 cup flaked coconut
¼ cup chopped nuts

Combine butter, sugar, cocoa and vanilla in double boiler. Cook over boiling water until blended. Carefully stir in egg and cook 3 minutes longer, stirring constantly. Stir in crumbs, coconut and nuts. Press into buttered 9-inch square pan. Cool.

*Second Layer*

½ cup butter
2 cups sifted confectioners'
  sugar

3 tablespoons milk
2 tablespoons instant vanilla
  pudding mix

Cream butter and sugar until light and fluffy. Beat in milk and pudding mix. Spread over first layer and let stand until firm.

*Third Layer*

1 6-ounce package semi-sweet
  chocolate pieces

1 tablespoon butter

Melt chocolate and butter together in double boiler over hot water. Spread over second layer. Cool until firm. Cut into small squares. Store in refrigerator.

Way back there in the Appetizers, we gave the recipe for Puffs or Pâté à Choux. When you want to use these for desserts, here are some fillings.

## WHIPPED CREAM FILLING

1 tablespoon gelatin
¼ cup water
1 cup whipping cream

2 tablespoons sugar
Flavorings: rum, brandy, coffee,
  vanilla, almond, etc.

*To keep raisins and other fruits evenly distributed in a batter, dust with flour before mixing them in.*

Soften gelatin in water and dissolve over hot water in a double boiler. Whip cream stiff with the sugar and fold in the gelatin mixture. Flavor as desired.

## CREAM PATISSERIE

| | |
|---|---|
| 1½ cups milk | ¼ cup flour |
| ½ cup sugar | ½ teaspoon vanilla |
| 4 egg yolks | |

Scald the milk. Mix the sugar and egg yolks together until creamy and smooth. Add the flour, blending just enough to be smooth. Add the scalded milk gradually until well combined. Return to heat and bring just to a boil, but do not let it boil. Add the vanilla. Strain and cool.

## CHOCOLATE CREAM PATISSERIE

Same as above but add two squares of unsweetened chocolate to the milk while scalding it.

## MOCHA CREAM PATISSERIE

Add ¼ cup ground coffee (can use instant) to scalded milk. Let stand 15 minutes. Strain and proceed as for Cream Patisserie.

## CREAM ST. HONORE

| | |
|---|---|
| 3 cups cream Patisserie | ¼ cup water |
| 1 envelope (1 tablespoon) | 6 egg whites |
| gelatin | ¼ cup sugar |

Soften gelatin in cold water and dissolve it over hot water and blend it into hot cream Patisserie. Whip the egg whites stiff, adding the sugar gradually to make a meringue. Fold it into the Patisserie mix.

---

*Raisins for cakes and breads will be plump and juicy if you soak them in warm water before adding to the batter.*

## COCKTAIL WALNUTS

For each cup of walnut meats:

| | |
|---|---|
| 1 tablespoon butter | ¼ teaspoon salt |
| ½ teaspoon chili powder | ¼ teaspoon onion salt |
| 1 teaspoon Worcestershire sauce | |

Blend seasonings into melted butter, then stir in walnuts until all are well coated. Spread nuts and melted butter into a thin layer in a shallow pan and bake in 300° oven for 25 minutes. Do not cover. Allow to cool on paper towel.

## MINTED NUTS

| | |
|---|---|
| 1 cup sugar | ½ teaspoon essence of pepper- |
| 1 tablespoon corn syrup | mint, or 3 drops oil of |
| ½ cup water | peppermint |
| ⅛ teaspoon salt | 3 cups walnuts |
| 6 marshmallows | |

Cook together the sugar, corn syrup, water and salt. Remove from heat when it forms a very soft ball when tested in cold water (230° on candy thermometer). Add marshmallows and stir until melted. Add peppermint and nuts and stir until every nut is covered and mixture hardens. Drop on paper, a teaspoonful at a time, to cool. These can be kept fresh in a tightly covered jar for at least a week.

## SUGARED NUTS

| | |
|---|---|
| 3 cups walnut meats | 4 tablespoons water |
| 1 teaspoon cinnamon | 1 pinch cream of tartar |
| 1 cup brown sugar | |

Cook ingredients (except nuts), in open saucepan until mixture forms a soft ball when dropped in cold water (230° on candy thermometer). Remove from fire and immediately stir in walnuts until all are coated. Spread into thin layer on wax paper or buttered plate. As soon as cool enough to handle, separate and allow to cool.

---

*To keep apples, pears and peaches from turning brown, put them in cold water to which a little lemon juice has been added.*

143

### SPICED SUGARED NUTS

1 ½ cups sugar
½ cup molasses
¼ cup water
1 tablespoon butter
1 teaspoon cinnamon

½ teaspoon ginger
½ teaspoon allspice
⅛ teaspoon cloves
¾ pound walnut meats

Mix sugar, molasses, water and butter in pan. Cook until small amount of syrup forms firm ball in cold water (230° on candy thermometer). Remove from heat. Add spices, and stir until syrup begins to grain. Add nuts. Continue stirring until nuts are coated and well grained. Before mixture hardens, separate each nut and cool on cookie sheet. Keep in tightly covered jar.

### KAHLUA UNDER THE SINK

2 cups water
4 cups sugar
2 ounce jar instant coffee

2 cups brandy
1 vanilla bean

Boil water. Mix sugar and coffee. Add boiling water. Cool, add brandy, pour into glass ½-gallon wine bottle. Drop in vanilla bean. Let stand 30 days *under the sink.*

### CHERRY BOOZE ON A HIGH, SAFE SHELF
### OR
### VISHNIAK

1 pound big, perfect Bing cherries
1 pound granulated sugar

1 fifth of gin, or vodka or brandy (90 proof if possible)

Wash and stem the cherries very gently so as not to bruise them. Dry on a towel. Place them in a clean 2-quart jar. Pour the pound of sugar over the cherries. DO NOT STIR OR SHAKE. Pour the liquor over the sugar and cherries. Do not stir. Cover with a lid. Put the jar on a high, safe shelf and let it stand three months. Strain into 2

*If you like your fried potatoes golden brown, sprinkle them lightly with flour before frying.*

144

1-quart bottles. The cherry meat will be dissolved and the color is "gorgeous" and the taste "divine" to quote Mrs. George Bearyman of Costa Mesa who says she's willing to stake her life on the validity and great quality and taste of this recipe. (This may be a variation of the plum liqueur, Vishniak.)

Another of Mrs. Lud Gluskin's favorites.


### SANGRIA (GRECO)

Prepare in a glass jug holding 2 quarts:

| | |
|---|---|
| 4 tablespoons of powdered sugar | ¾ glass of Cointreau |
| 1 liqueur (1½ ounces) glass of Cognac | Juice of ½ lemon |
| ½ liqueur glass of red Curaçao | Peel of one whole lemon |
| | 1 bottle dry red wine (fifth) |

Shake for one minute. Add 1 bottle of dry red wine. Add ice and finish by filling the jug with soda water. Shake and drink.


### BOURBON PUNCH

| | |
|---|---|
| 1 quart bourbon | 1 quart ginger ale |
| 1 quart white grape juice | ½ quart sparkling water |

Place a large chunk of ice in punch bowl. Add ingredients.


### CHAMPAGNE PUNCH

| | |
|---|---|
| ½ cup lemon juice | 3 ounces Curaçao |
| ½ cup water | 3 ounces maraschino |
| 1 cup sugar | 1 bottle sparkling water |
| 3 ounces brandy | 3 bottles Champagne |

In punch bowl, dissolve sugar in water and lemon juice. Add brandy, Curaçao, and maraschino. Mix well. Just before serving, pour in chilled sparkling water and Champagne. Stir gently. Garnish with fresh strawberries or pineapple.

145

## POLYNESIAN PUNCH

½ quart Sweet and Sour (buy it at your liquor store or make a simple syrup by boiling together equal parts sugar and water and combining equal parts of the syrup with lemon juice)

1 quart Mai Tai mix
1 quart Scorpion mix
½ quart orange juice
2 quarts sparkling water
2 fifths light rum

Place a block of ice in punch bowl and pour ingredients over. Mix well and float pineapple sticks or flowers on it.

## SCREWDRIVER PUNCH

1 quart orange juice
1 quart sparkling water

½ quart quinine water
1 fifth vodka

Place a block of ice in punch bowl and pour ingredients over. Mix well. Float orange or lemon slices on top.

# The Words at the End

And so let us end as we began—Softly now.

Never in the history of man has there been a nation as affluent as ours. Never before in history has there been a nation with the leisure time we enjoy. Let's hear a final word from Dr. Dichter. Human happiness does not mean that all incentives be directed toward filling one's stomach. It actually means the exact opposite. Only if we have some fairly good assurance that we are going to have enough to eat do we become free enough to devote ourselves to higher, more important goals. The modern housewife who does not have to spend most of her day in preparing food, carrying water and firing the oven has the time and leisure to devote her energies to more inspiring pursuits. Whether she does this, or utilizes her new-found leisure for meaningless activities, only time and the scientific study of human behavior will tell. We must adapt ourselves to the future. We have been confronted with the problem of leisure in a world of plenty. The answer does not lie in forcing people back into slavery and hard work just because insisting that people work hard makes us feel moral. Nor does it lie in permitting people to use this new leisure for mental enslavement. A challenge has been posed which must be accepted. It is the job of the educator, the public servant, the communicator, the psychologist and the strategist of human desire to convince people to utilize this Freedom From Want for the pursuit of real happiness. And now,

> May the Road rise before you,
> The wind blow gently upon your back,
> The sun shine brightly upon your face,
> And the rains fall softly upon your fields.
> And, until we meet again,
> May God hold you in the hollow of his hand.

# Index

149